PRAISE FOR *USE YOUR PLANETS WISELY*

"I first met Jennifer two years ago when I was at a bit of a crossroads in my own life—I have a lot of access to special people with special abilities at Goop, but Jennifer cut through. My session with her, which I transcribed and documented, was transformative: She explained what was available to me—in a deeply personal and resonant way—and then coached me on how to step into my destiny. I see and speak to her regularly, and she's become a close friend. It has been thrilling to see how she has touched and transformed the lives of Goop readers in the same way over the past two years—her version of astrology, grounded in psychology, has the ability to force needed change in a profound way."

ELISE LOEHNEN
chief content officer, Goop

"Jennifer is an incredibly brilliant astrologer who uniquely combines her understanding of the stars with her deep background as a practical therapist. I've been seeing Jennifer Freed for over 15 years and her guidance is truly priceless. She teaches us that our path is not only about destiny, but how to experience the highest version of reality available for each of our souls' unique paths and journeys here in Earth school. In short, she has helped me transform on every level and I know her offering will help you step into your power and align with your greatest gifts."

LAUREN ROXBURGH
bestselling author and wellness educator

"Dr. Jen Freed brilliantly blends the art, heart, and science of relationship, career, and life advice. She is the closest thing to having a wise angel for guidance on your path in life. Whereas traditional coaches, therapists, and counselors can take weeks to get baseline information only to start digging into your case, Jen's experience and unparalleled skillset of tapping into ancient science allows her to get to the root of your life within one session. Change your life for the better with Dr. Freed's beautiful wisdom."

DR. WILL COLE
leading functional medicine expert
and bestselling author of *Ketotarian*
and *The Inflammation Spectrum*

"Jennifer Freed is a clear vessel for understanding ourselves and others with profound compassion. Learning from her to how to interpret the planets and the signs was life-changing."

MARCIA CROSS
award-winning actress

"Jennifer is a powerful combination of compassion, clarity, and insight."

BOYD VARTY
author of *Cathedral of the Wild*
and *The Lion Tracker's Guide to Life*

"Jennifer masterfully combines psychology and astrology to empower each individual to harness their uniqueness. She shares her wisdom and experience in a direct and accessible way which encourages each of us to celebrate our gifts and transform our challenges into strengths. She is a beacon of truth and her work helps illuminate the way forward for us all!"

MARY AND LUCY FIRESTONE
founders of Firestone Sisters, Inc.

USE YOUR PLANETS WISELY

Master Your
Ultimate Cosmic
Potential with
Psychological Astrology

USE YOUR PLANETS WISELY

JENNIFER FREED, PHD

sounds true
BOULDER, COLORADO

Sounds True
Boulder, CO 80306

Individual stories are shared in this book for illustrative purposes. Names and
identifying details have been changed to protect the privacy of those individuals.

Published 2020

Cover design by Jennifer Miles
Book design by Beth Skelley

Sample Birth Chart on p. 14 by Molly Green

Printed in Canada

Library of Congress Cataloging-in-Publication Data

Names: Freed, Jennifer, 1958- author.
Title: Use your planets wisely : master your ultimate cosmic potential with
    psychological astrology / by Jennifer Freed, Ph.D.
Description: Boulder, CO : Sounds True, 2019.
Identifiers: LCCN 2019013297 (print) | LCCN 2019016352 (ebook) | ISBN
    9781683644439 (hardcover)
Subjects: LCSH: Astrology and psychology.
Classification: LCC BF1729.P8 F74 2019 (print) | LCC BF1729.P8 (ebook) |
    DDC 133.5--dc23
LC record available at https://lccn.loc.gov/2019013297
LC ebook record available at https://lccn.loc.gov/2019016352

Ebook ISBN: 978-1-68364-444-6

10 9 8 7 6 5 4 3 2 1

To the divine muses
who have honored me
with oracular gifts.

CONTENTS

the bonfire

Mars represents the power of will and the force of action. Knowing where Mars falls in the birth chart helps you work with your gifts to achieve your goals and dreams and lets you know what pitfalls are most likely to disrupt your ability to act and do. The placement of Mars, sometimes nicknamed "the angry planet," affects your assertiveness, your expression of anger, your athletic drives, and the more yang (masculine) expressions of your sexuality.

the high mountain lake

Jupiter represents expansion, growth, and success. It also represents generosity, honor, abundance, pride, and optimism. Its placement in the birth chart says a lot about how you express—or overexpress or struggle to express—these qualities in your life.

the mountain

Saturn represents structure, time, and tradition. It balances the expansive energy of Jupiter with necessary limitation and realism. The placement of Saturn in the signs speaks to not only how you make order from chaos but also how you are limited by boundaries. Saturn gets a bad rap—it's sometimes symbolized as a skeleton, turning your thoughts toward mortality and the inevitability of death. But without a skeleton, you'd be nothing but a pile of flesh and viscera. You need your skeleton to stand and walk and do all you do, just as you need the structure of Saturn to manifest, to stay grounded, to persist and work hard.

The Pluto archetype represents primordial energy and deep transformation. Its placement in your chart helps you understand your impulses to go as deep as a human being can go; to tell the truth, no matter what the consequences; to dive into the mysteries of sex, birth, and death. This understanding can help you manage impulses toward hatred, greed, jealousy, and lust—which *everyone* has because there is a Pluto placement in every chart—and channel those drives into creativity and into the kind of transformation that is beneficial in the long run (even if disruptive and difficult in the short term).

PREFACE

How to Use This Book

You hold in your hands one of the most powerful tools available for understanding yourself and other human beings. In the following pages, you will have access to the DNA of the cosmos and the sacred map of the psyche.

You are receiving a magnificent gift, and with it comes an ethical responsibility. The knowledge in this book will give you what you need to dramatically transform your relationship to yourself and others—a laser-like insight into what makes *you* tick and into what truly motivates others. It is the quickest way to build lasting empathy and to surrender the judgments that separate human beings from one another.

Like any cosmic force, the wisdom in this book can be misused by those who hold misaligned intentions. The fact that this book has come into your possession means you are ready for rapid growth and to be a beacon for others who wish to join you in that trajectory. The knowledge shared here can be mined throughout an entire lifetime; the deeper you engage the material and use the practices, the more wisdom you will receive.

As you commit to the integrity of these devotional messages and to the practices that make them personal to you, you will notice a huge uptick in cosmic support. You will actually be able to feel and sense a magnification of your connection to the divine.

Personal stories in this book (with names and details altered to protect people's privacy) reveal how each of us has the capacity to evolve at any age and to radically change and upgrade our psychological and spiritual operating systems. Used correctly, this book can offer you unlimited growth. Here is what you need in order to use this potent knowledge:

1. Obtain a printout of your birth chart that includes all the planets, Chiron, and your rising sign. You can find these for free from online apps like Time Passages or Co-Star or the website astro.com. Enter your birth date, time, and place. (If you do not know your birth time, you should enter 12:00 p.m.; your rising sign will be inaccurate, and your Moon sign may not be accurate either, but the rest will be.) If you would like to purchase a more comprehensive and detailed report on your planets to use with this book please email useyourplanetswisely@gmail.com and Dr. Jennifer Freed will reply within 24 hours.

2. Once you have a chart or listing of all your planetary placements and rising sign, write them out—for example: Sun in Gemini, Moon in Taurus, Mercury in Gemini, and so on. Most sites that generate birth charts will also generate general descriptions of the meaning of your planets' sign placement; you can review those as a starting point if you like.

RULES OF ENGAGEMENT

Once you have your printout and general notes in hand, review these ground rules:

1. Use this book when you have undistracted, focused time when you can not only read the information but

also keenly *feel* what is being shared. Find a special place to read where your spiritual attention feels enhanced.

2. Read only what you are called to in the moment. Go slowly. Take in small bits at a time. This is a rich meal that must be digested with care.

3. Take *only* your *own* inventory in terms of analyzing Primitive, Adaptive, and Evolving levels of application. You are the only person you can change; there is only power in working on yourself. Keep your eyes on your own road of growth!

4. If you choose to look at someone else's planets, use the information you find only to encourage and appreciate them. They are the only ones who can or should use this material to make a critical inventory or comment on their own level of application.

5. Speak from your heart; listen with your heart. The only true spiritual purpose that unites us all is love. Start with loving yourself now.

6. Do the practices. Like any discipline, this one will only gift you as much as you put in. Even if you only do one chapter a month and really *do* the exercises, you will gain far more benefit than if you hurry through. Because psychological astrology is constantly revealing nuances and sparks of insight as you progress and learn, you can delve into any chapter again and again over a lifetime.

This final point deserves a bit more explanation. In doing these exercises with others who are also using this book, you will expand your individual learning into a web of community. You will be an active part of building a network of conscious allies as you work to be your most fully realized, brilliantly expressed self, and you will also have the opportunity to be an ally to others. This is how we begin to build a community that is about self-acceptance, self-realization, and accountability to a greater scope than our own egoic concerns. This is how we begin to heal the rifts that have arisen as we've set sail on our own rafts of individual interests, forgetting that the truest and most enduring gifts we can possess are those we discover and cultivate as a collective.

INTRODUCTION

Psychological Astrology: An Ancient Science for the Modern Age

If you think of yourself as simply a Virgo or a Pisces or a Capricorn, be prepared to expand your self-knowledge many times over as I guide you through a deep understanding of the sign placement of the significant cosmic archetypes in your birth chart.

Your birth chart reveals at least *ten times* more about you than you might have thought. And while some of these additional insights are echoes of your Sun sign, others are likely to reflect parts of yourself that represent radical departures from that sign. In other words, if you only know your Sun sign, you have only just begun to understand your birth chart. The knowledge in this book will give you a far more complete picture of your psychological and emotional blueprint.

This book is for everyone who would like to better know themselves, have better relationships, and enjoy greater happiness and fulfillment in community. It's not just for those who are already fans of astrology and have some knowledge; it's also for skeptics.

WHY SHOULD I CARE ABOUT MORE THAN MY SUN SIGN?

A typical daily horoscope column gives a thumbnail sketch about your Sun sign, which is the sign that was in the sky above your birthplace on the day of your birth. Giving total credence to this snapshot is like seeing a single photo of a person and thinking you know what they look like from every angle, in every possible light, in every outfit and every mood. The Sun sign is an important piece of a person's makeup, but it's only one factor in the complex and instructive full complement of planets and signs. Consider these examples:

Pip is a Sun sign Virgo. This placement typically describes a person who excels at industry, perfectionism, utility, and service. This is all true about Pip, but what you *wouldn't* know by looking at her Sun sign is that she has a Moon in Cancer, which is one of the most highly sensitive, needy, clingy, emotional constitutions a person can have. Her rising sign is Libra, which confers upon her the capacity to be exceedingly beautiful and charming and to use diplomacy as a way to open all doors. Her Mars is in Leo, which enables her to soar in the performing arts as an expressive film and stage star.

Claire has her Sun in Capricorn, which is a placement known for its dependability, reliability, ambition, and sturdiness. What that doesn't say about Claire is that her Aquarius rising makes her a friend to all and a person who can rock highly eccentric outfits! In addition, Claire has Mars and Saturn in Sagittarius; this makes her a prolific teacher of joy—a person with the capacity for disciplined and abundant partying.

Imagine your whole personality as a mobile with many parts. A single part of this mobile cannot describe the entirety of who you are, and each of the various parts can be quite different! Recognizing and honoring those parts is the key to coordinating them to work together as a vibrant whole.

MERGING ASTROLOGY, PSYCHOLOGY, AND SOCIAL-EMOTIONAL LEARNING

I've been practicing and teaching psychological astrology for more than thirty years. Since I discovered astrology in the 1970s, I've been captivated by its wisdom and power. As soon as I began to read about it and learn from my teacher, Dr. Richard Tarnas,[1] I knew it would always be an abiding passion of mine. I learned to generate birth charts without a computer (no small feat, but that's how we had to do it back then, before computer programs made chart generation simple and easy). I read everything I could get my hands on and began to do readings as soon as I felt skilled enough. All these years later, I still find that as a comprehensive system for understanding individual human beings in the context of an intelligent universe, astrology has no competition.

I have spent just as many years studying and practicing depth psychology, which—with its focus on subjective, personal experience; the power of story and mythology; and the collective unconscious—is a good fit with astrology. I have had the exquisite privilege of spending my professional life practicing psychology and psychotherapy with individuals, couples, and groups, as well as working as a psychology professor at Pacifica Graduate Institute and Antioch University and social-emotional educator through AHA!, the organization I cofounded (ahasb.org).

What do I mean by *psychological astrology*? It is a little-understood, dynamic practice that brings together depth psychology and astrology along their unifying thread: both are about understanding our potentials and challenges and about moving, through self-knowledge and practice, into more constructive ways of being and relating.

Who am I, really? What did I come here to do? How am I meant to realize my potential? In what areas am I weakest, and how can I fortify myself in those areas? How can I best care for myself? How can I solve my most pressing problems? Who am I in relationship? What are my needs, and what is most mine to give? What could be my greatest contribution or legacy in my lifetime? A good therapist will help you answer these questions; so will a good astrologer. I have the privilege of deeply understanding both areas of practice, and I have had much success in combining them in my work with individuals and groups. My psychotherapy training has given me a rich understanding of the ways in which biographic and emotional material can interfere with or support present-moment astrological insight.

One important goal of psychological exploration is the integration of all the parts of the self, including parts that have been rejected, ignored, or suppressed. We all have parts like these. By identifying the patterns, beliefs, and needs that show up in the birth chart, we make what is *un*conscious, conscious. As we bring all these parts forward into the light, look at them as what they are, and accept and integrate them, we become happier, more whole, and more *ourselves*. We come to better understand where and how we fit into our intimate relationships, communities, and cultures. My approach as both psychotherapist and astrologer has always focused on identifying strengths and working with them, rather than on pathologizing and diagnosing; this positive psychological slant informs the material in this book.

What about social-emotional learning? What is it, and where does this fit into the picture of what I'm offering here?

Social-emotional learning focuses on knowing how to name and manage our emotions, delay gratification, and show grit and temerity in reaching our goals, as well as on knowing how to repair conflict and how to reach out for help where needed. No matter how great our self-understanding, we need practice and awareness to effectively express and manage our emotions, empathize, engage in self-care, listen well, communicate effectively, and repair relationship problems. Without this, it can be all too easy to use our birth chart's archetypal blueprint as a justification for bad behavior ("I didn't mean to yell at you, but I can't help it with three planets in Aries!") rather than as a guide for skillful interactions and service to the world. It's too easy to retreat into ourselves rather than connect with others in a meaningful way. And once we start to build a working knowledge of astrology, it's tempting to use *others'* charts to make assumptions about what they are and are not capable of or whether it's worth our effort to connect with them deeply.

Most self-help books focus on getting you what *you* want, making *your* fortune, realizing *your* potential, chasing *your* dreams, being a rugged individualist who does it *your* way. In a world where most people are used to having it their way—the music they like, the newsfeed that supports their beliefs, the clothes that express the self—polishing one's personal identity and chasing personal achievement are held as the highest aims.

Yet, the idea that we thrive most when we take responsibility for and rely upon only ourselves has become a huge source of sadness and disconnection. And disconnection and loneliness are literally killing us: the loneliness that is epidemic in Western society now has been found to be more dangerous to our health than being obese or smoking fifteen cigarettes a day.

This book helps begin the way back from a state of alienation to a place where living out our own gifts and talents is not only about lifting ourselves up but also about building connection and strength for all. Social-emotional learning is, ultimately, about how we relate to each other, and that's why it is an imperative part of the work in this book. This idea is so important to me that with my partner Rendy Freedman, MFT, a therapist and educator, I began delivering social-emotional learning to teenagers, families, and educators through AHA!, a nonprofit organization we cofounded in 1999. Since then, AHA!'s staff of skilled facilitators—all of whom Rendy and I have trained and supervised—has educated more than 20,000 people in high schools, out-of-school (after-school and summer) programs, parent groups, and educator and administrator trainings in schools in Southern California and at conferences nationwide.

The social and emotional pieces are absolutely necessary to make the best possible use of the information found in a birth chart. While your birth chart is about *you*, it's also about your place in the grand scheme of things. While psychological and astrological self-understanding and social-emotional mastery will definitely make *you* happier and get *you* more of what you want and need, they also are vital for you to be an effective part of building a world that's better for everyone.

Once any of us delve deeply enough into our own archetypal nature and its connection to universal themes, we become more available to help others find their way. We see how we are alike in ways that have nothing to do with our small ego concerns. We become more accepting of differences between people. Through understanding our planetary placements, we get clear about how we can be useful and meaningful to others around us. We need social and emotional skills to do this well.

We don't come into this world knowing how to be with each other or how to feel and express emotions in healthy ways. We learn from what we see—from our parents, from our culture, from our media. And most would agree that there are a *lot* of bad social and emotional examples out there. Most people can benefit from social-emotional education and ongoing practice in improving these intelligences—practical learning about how to be an effective, empathic, trustworthy, growthful, emotionally healthy, creative, collaborative, connected human being. Modern educational and psychological research supports this strongly, and workplaces and schools nationwide are implementing processes and programs to promote social-emotional intelligence. The practices in this book are directly created to strengthen your social and emotional skills.

In my work with thousands of clients, I have seen how this approach of combining astrology, psychology, and social-emotional learning has a kind of impact I have not seen with any one of these disciplines alone. Any one of these three areas of study and practice will, with people who are willing and want to change for the better, create improvement. But bringing all three together builds an incredible alchemy: these people come to understand their own inner workings, to see both their uniqueness and their commonalities with others, and to break destructive habits of self-talk and relationship. They achieve a level of self-actualization and a deep joy and satisfaction that radiate from who they are. They come to trust that there is a divine orchestration that guides them, that they have a purpose in the world, and that both their light and their shadows are welcome participants in their psychological and relational lives.

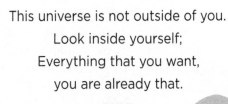

This universe is not outside of you.
Look inside yourself;
Everything that you want,
you are already that.

RUMI

1

WELCOME to the
NEW PARADIGM of
PSYCHOLOGICAL
ASTROLOGY

You are about to take a voyage into a way of knowing yourself that will yield an intricate, detailed portrait of who you are: the good, the bad, the spectacular, the parts you'd rather remain hidden, the beautiful, the ugly.

As a dual practitioner of psychology and astrology, I have come to believe that the desire to know the self completely can lead to the most magical journey possible in this life. Astrology lends vivid description to what makes you, you. It helps you see how you are part of everything and how everything is part of you. In seeing this and in having a desire to be the best version of you that you can be—the one with the kind of relationships that feel congruent with your values, doing the work that matters to you and that feeds your soul—you will be able to actualize those parts in the best possible way.

This book will guide you in understanding your full astrological birth chart. The purpose is to help you see yourself clearly: both your favorite parts—the ones you lead with any time you enter a room with other people in it—and your less favorite parts, some of which might just be underused or under-recognized and some of which you might actively hide and feel ashamed of because you don't know how to use them in a way that helps and does not hurt.

Maybe you didn't know astrology could do this, especially if you have only looked at the meaning of your Sun sign to understand what your astrological blueprint says about who you are. So, before we go deeper . . .

A NOTE FOR SKEPTICS

If you think astrology is bunk and picked this book up anyway, thank you, and good for you. You chose to go outside of what you already think to be true. You are inviting something strange and new into your life. I wish more people were like you in that way! Even if you don't get past this first chapter, know that you have already done something more daring than many others will ever do.

Your skepticism may come from having only ever read your Sun sign horoscope. Maybe sometimes that horoscope has been right on target; maybe other times you've felt no connection to it at all. It might have only taken a couple of times seeing that your horoscope didn't reflect your experience for you to dismiss astrology altogether.

Some folks dismiss astrology without a second look because it lacks the kind of scientific support we have come to expect from our systems for bettering ourselves. Consider that scientific methods cannot capture everything. If you are new to astrology, try to stay open to the joy and wonder that lie beyond what you think you know. See for yourself if it speaks to you. As you read, ask yourself: *Does this material excite my mind? Does it fill my heart? Does it make me feel something in my body? Does it feel true? Does it feel useful? Does it make sense?*

If it does, that's all the evidence you need.

I think of astrology more as a romance art than as a science. It's actually a mytho-poetic tradition in which we recognize—just like the greatest experiences of life, like love and ecstasy—that it cannot be quantified but is truly profound.

SO MUCH MORE THAN SUN SIGNS

You may not have known that there is exponentially more to be seen and learned from your birth chart than the information conveyed by your sun sign. The Sun is only one of many planetary energies in your chart, and every single one of them occurs in an astrological sign. In every one of those planet-sign relationships lies a wealth of information about the strengths and liabilities of being *you*. Fully knowing your birth chart means coming to know, in intimate detail, your "inner committee"—those voices and influences inside of you that create either havoc and mayhem or success and contentment—and seeing ways to move up the ladder of skillfulness in every realm of your complex being.

Who are these inner committee members, and what do they have to say about your ultimate potentials and capacities? In coming to understand your planets' placement in the astrological signs, you will be able to answer this question. Each planet represents one aspect of your psychological/spiritual DNA. When you are able to understand each of these influences and know how to bring them to fruition and ultimate expression, you will see the way to personal happiness illuminated.

In learning to work with this inner committee, you will also become more skillful, strategic, and expert at working with others' inner committees—not in a manipulative, selfish way but in the spirit of recognizing, accepting, and celebrating the ways in which we are all different from and complementary to one another.

When you interact with others, it's *your* inner committee interacting with *theirs*. It's more like a dinner party, with all the personalities and proclivities clashing and merging, than like a one-on-one conversation. The knowledge you'll obtain in this book will support you in navigating this experience and enjoying it rather than wishing others would think, behave, and be more like you.

This is compassion and empathy in action: taking the time and putting in the effort to understand the many facets of yourself and others.

BIRTH CHART ASTROLOGY:
A VERY BASIC INTRODUCTION

Your birth chart is an abstracted "map" of the heavens snapped at the moment of your birth, showing the location of the planets in the sky from the vantage point of your birthplace. Each planet falls within a particular segment of the birth chart mandala.

The planets you will learn about in this book—the Sun, the Moon, Mercury, Mars, Venus, Jupiter, Saturn, Uranus, Neptune, and Pluto—are designated by the symbols you see around the outer edge of the circle, which is divided into twelve sections. An asteroid, Chiron, which is also important to recognize and understand in the birth chart, is included as well. A chapter is also devoted to the *rising sign*. Also known as the *ascendant*, the rising sign is the sign that was on the horizon at the moment of your birth.

Each planet in the birth chart represents a specific *archetype*. In astrology, an archetype represents what my teacher, Richard Tarnas, calls "a universal principle or force that affects—impels, structures, permeates—the human psyche and human behavior on many levels."[2] In other words, each planet is connected to specific psychological, social, and emotional expressions. The Sun represents the archetype of identity; the Moon, of personal needs and habits; Mercury, of communication; Venus, of love and beauty; Mars, of action and the force of will; Jupiter, of expansion; Saturn, of structure and discipline; Uranus, of rebellion and innovation; Neptune, of the dissolving of boundaries and universal consciousness; Pluto, of depth and transformation; and the asteroid Chiron, of the wounded healer.

In a birth chart, each planet falls into the realm of one of the twelve astrological signs, each of which occupies about a month of the yearly calendar. Most people are familiar with these signs from Sun sign newspaper horoscopes: Aries, Taurus, Gemini,

A SAMPLE BIRTH CHART

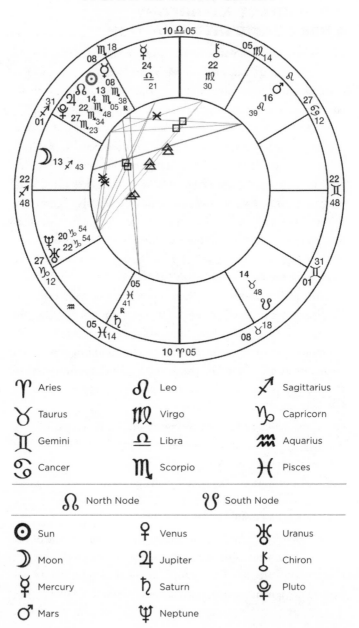

♈ Aries	♌ Leo	♐ Sagittarius
♉ Taurus	♍ Virgo	♑ Capricorn
♊ Gemini	♎ Libra	♒ Aquarius
♋ Cancer	♏ Scorpio	♓ Pisces

☊ North Node	☋ South Node

☉ Sun	♀ Venus	♅ Uranus
☽ Moon	♃ Jupiter	⚷ Chiron
☿ Mercury	♄ Saturn	♇ Pluto
♂ Mars	♆ Neptune	

Cancer, Leo, Virgo, Libra, Scorpio, Sagittarius, Capricorn, Aquarius, and Pisces. In the sample chart, you can see the symbols for these signs sitting just inward of their planets toward the center of the circle (with a number between them).

Over millennia, ancient astrologers came to recognize certain characteristics and qualities that tended to emerge and reemerge in people with certain placements of planets in the signs. As those astrologers gathered and distilled what they learned, wisdom was passed down and recorded. This is the wisdom astrologers continue to draw on and reinforce in modern times.[3]

All of the planetary archetypes exist in every person, "clothed" in the look, feel, and expressive qualities of one of the astrological signs. An astrologer can "read" a lot about a person from their birth chart based on the placement of each planet within the astrological signs. Just to give a few examples of the impact the signs might have on the planets:

Jeffrey, whose Sun is in Cancer, is a sensitive man who is great with children and cries easily. The archetype of the Sun is expressed in Jeffrey through the emotional, tender, familial lens of the sign of Cancer.

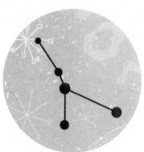

Monica's Uranus is in Taurus, which might mean her tendency to rebel and innovate (the archetypal expression of Uranus) plays out in the form of material, earthy pursuits. She likes to grow gorgeous gardens with unexpected combinations of plants, and she decorates her home with unique and sensual objects.

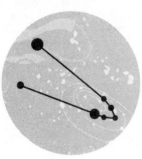

Can't figure out why your beloved is so secretive about their emotions, while you want to shout your love and rage to the rooftops? Once you recognize that your Moon is in Aries and their Moon is in Scorpio, you'll have an easier time accepting and navigating that difference. You'll even be able to predict what their needs might be in a given situation and tell them how to predict yours.

Your Sun in Sagittarius might be the reason you sometimes come across as insensitive or bossy to your close friend, whose Sun is in Pisces; it might also be the reason your Pisces Sun friend is so emotional about things and sometimes has difficulty showing up on time and focused when you make plans to hang out.

This is the kind of expertise readers of *Use Your Planets Wisely* will develop: the ability to understand the ways these archetypes are expressed in themselves and others and how they are likely to affect behavior and relationships. This knowledge both inspires compassion and brings personal and interpersonal power.

To see how planets are placed in signs, read the sample chart counterclockwise from below the horizontal line at the left side (the rising line). Neptune and Uranus are in Capricorn; Saturn is in Pisces; Mars is in Leo; Chiron is in Virgo; Mercury is in Libra; Venus, the Sun, Jupiter, and Pluto are in Scorpio; and the Moon is in Sagittarius. The sign to the outside left of the rising line is the rising sign or ascendant; here, that sign is Sagittarius.

The lines and symbols that *aren't* the planets and the signs—that is, the lines through the center with the squares, triangles, and asterisks (the *aspects*) and the two symbols that resemble horseshoes that sit directly across from each other (the *nodes*)—are beyond the scope of this book.

This book is meant to do the following:

- Provide an easy, simple way to understand your own birth chart or the birth charts of others.

- Change your life immediately by bringing clarity to your multiple parts, in all their complexities, including your "blind spots," or the parts of yourself you cannot or don't want to see clearly. (I'll do this in a way that brings hope and positive change, not hopelessness and resignation.)

- Show you how differently these maps are composed for every different person.

- Help you shift from walking around misjudging others, secretly thinking, *they're just like me—they just don't know it; why can't they do as I would do, or as I think they should do?* to a deep understanding and appreciation of inborn differences and differences in expression.

- Show you how to use your talents and find workable ways to improve in areas with more growth potential.

- Encourage you to bring your best to your community and the world.

"LEVELING" PLANETS WITHIN THE SIGNS

In my thirty years of consulting with clients worldwide, I've come to recognize that everyone moves through identifiable stages of psychological and cosmic development. These stages are not linear; they are more like a gradually climbing spiral. I wanted a less linear, more nuanced, less "good vs. bad" way to talk about the potential of each sign in each planet than is usually found in astrology books and teachings. I wanted to use descriptions of each planet's expression within the signs that allow for the fact that we all, at any time, can feel driven to act and interact in less mature ways, especially if we do not remain conscious of the forces that drive us. I wanted to empower us all, at any time, to choose to become more aware of these forces and use them wisely.

This is the first book on astrology that describes the psychological *levels* of the planets in the signs—that is, it looks at each planet in each sign in terms of different levels of skillful and unskillful expression. Each of the chapters addressing the planets (Sun, Moon, Mercury, Mars, Venus, Jupiter, Uranus, Saturn, Neptune, Pluto, and the asteroid Chiron) includes the following:

- A description of the *origin myth* of the planet being described

- An *updated, nature-based symbol* for that planet that captures the same archetypal energies[4]

- A description of *three levels* at which the energies represented by that planet in each sign of the birth chart can be expressed

PRIMITIVE We all are wired to express reptilian, survival-oriented strategies. When we refuse to acknowledge them—when we cloak them in shame and regard them with fear—we end up living them out unconsciously, often in unskillful or harmful ways. Let's all admit that every one of us carries this primitive, regressive, developmentally delayed patterning. Instead of trying to bury or banish it, we need to find ways to bring out those parts of ourselves in safe settings where they can be nurtured and healed—where they can be transformed rather than acted out.

ADAPTIVE Once we've recognized our lower vibratory impulses, we can systematically raise our potential to be more functional and adaptive to more mature, adult-centered interactions with the self and others. We are taking the ladder up from the reptilian brain to engage the neocortex in decision-making and deliberation; our motivations become more thoughtful, reflective, and considerate of others' needs.

EVOLVING When we realize that our best interest is always embedded in the highest good for all, the question that predominates is, *how may my love/talent/gifts serve the collective?* In this highest expression of planetary and zodiacal archetypes, the primary motivation becomes one of contribution. At this level of expression, it becomes possible to transmute energy or be present in a way that can instantly transform others.

Psychological astrology does not shame people for the levels they are able to achieve because all of life is seen as a lesson plan. No one in this cosmology has mastered their lessons; if they had, they simply would not have incarnated. Through the format in this book, you can learn to easily laugh at yourself when you recognize yourself acting out the Primitive level of a planet in a sign; you can also have great discussions with others about how to move into the Adaptive and Evolving levels.

It's not possible to always live out an Evolving version of the planetary archetypes. We all swing back to the Primitive and through the Adaptive throughout our lives. The Primitive expressions described for each sign in each planet exist for everyone. In fact, we *all* experience them, and they *require* expression. We all know what happens when we pretend we have no shadow sides: the unrecognized, unexpressed shadow often ends up taking over.

Through this book's knowledge and practices, you will learn not to achieve some ongoing pinnacle of perfect expression of the potentials in your birth chart; rather, you will learn to increasingly inhabit the Adaptive and Evolving qualities of your planets and notice and forgive yourself (and others) quickly when the Primitive mode takes the lead.

Within each chapter, I describe the Primitive, Adaptive, and Evolving possibilities of the featured planet in each of the twelve astrological signs. Lots of real-life examples (shared anonymously, with names and details changed) are provided. Here are a couple examples that show how these levels can operate:

Ben, whose Sun is in Pisces and who has his Moon and rising signs in Scorpio (all of which are water signs), worked with me for years to get out of codependent relationships. In those relationships, he was always the doormat and would periodically fall into addictive heroin use out of wanting to escape emotional pain. Ben was rarely able to rise above the Primitive application of his planets in the signs.

Leandra has her Sun in Cancer, Moon in Scorpio, and Pisces rising. For reasons you will likely understand as you work through this book, these placements of water signs in these important locations on the birth chart could mean Primitive challenges for Leandra similar to what Ben faced. But she channeled her great capacities for feeling and empathy into starting an organization supporting orphaned children and is known as one of the warmest, kindest leaders in her field. She is a prime example of living most of the time at the Evolving level.

DEEP LEARNING AND INTEGRATION THROUGH SOCIAL-EMOTIONAL PRACTICES

Each chapter addressing a planetary archetype ends with practices drawn from social-emotional learning—practices that will deepen your personal understanding of that planet for yourself, as well as encourage connection with others. These practices are Dive In, Reach Out, Risk It, and Reflect.

The last section of each chapter includes several question prompts designed for circle discussion with a book club, class, or friend or family gathering. My hope is that you will have at least one friend or loved one in your life who is willing to join in this adventure with you by reading the book and working through the practices and circle questions. If this isn't available to you, you can use a journal to engage in the practices and answer the questions solo.

The practices, which can be used daily, monthly, or yearly, are ideal for book-club activities or as a way to build intimacy in partnerships. The more the practices are implemented, the more they will enhance both personal happiness and deep connection. Modern neuroscience confirms that activities like these, practiced regularly, can literally "rewire" the brain to transform habitual ways of thinking and interacting.

A REVISED MYTHOLOGY

In traditional astrology, the planetary archetypes are usually described in terms of ancient Greek or Roman mythology. This book provides the archetypes with a much-needed updating and a grounding in the imagery of the natural world. For example, instead of referring to the myth of Apollo to describe the archetype of the Sun, I use the image of the taproot, a plant root with a fat central downward thrust and slender outgrowths. Instead of the limited feminine ancient myth of the goddess Venus, that archetype is described here as a lush but orderly garden.

By paying close attention to your inner operating instructions, you can milk the most out of your life and also be the biggest contribution to others. The knowledge in this book will not take away suffering and loss, as these are natural experiences in everyone's life; however, it will give you a big advantage at making the most out of what you have been given and will help you rise up from even the most difficult life situations. This book is for people who know that life is an awesome journey for which it helps to have a sacred and animated map.

KNOW THYSELF, HELP THYSELF, HELP OTHERS, HELP THE WORLD

I've enjoyed learning and practicing this amazing art of psychological astrology so much, and I feel confident that whoever commits to learning some basics and applying them will see their lives transform in all kinds of unexpected ways. However, this is not the kind of book that promises to catapult you from a life of stress, strain, anguish, and unrealized dreams to a life of sparkling success—if only you follow its instructions to the letter. Instead, it is the kind of book that works its magic through introducing the self to its full complexity and splendor.

As we more and more deeply discover ourselves, we come to better understand others. We come to accept others for who they are and to recognize the depth and breadth of what that really means—they have within them just as much richness and inner diversity as we do, and their makeup is not wrong just because it isn't like our own. We can show up for them fully ourselves, and they can trust that they can do the same with us.

Knowing ourselves deeply guides us right to the threshold of our life's purpose. We have all had others tell us what *they* think we should do, how we should be, what we're best equipped for. Psychological astrology helps us know this for ourselves with realizations that resonate deeply.

As we embrace who we really are—not who we think we should want to be—a light shines to show us the way. Maybe we don't see the fullness of where we're going, but we know in which direction we are better off taking our next steps. We can know that the rest will be revealed if we keep going, carrying our self-knowledge with us like a high-powered flashlight.

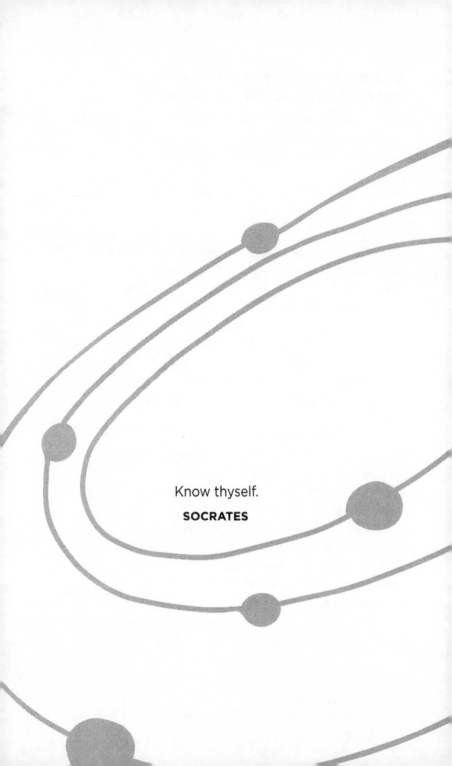

Know thyself.

SOCRATES

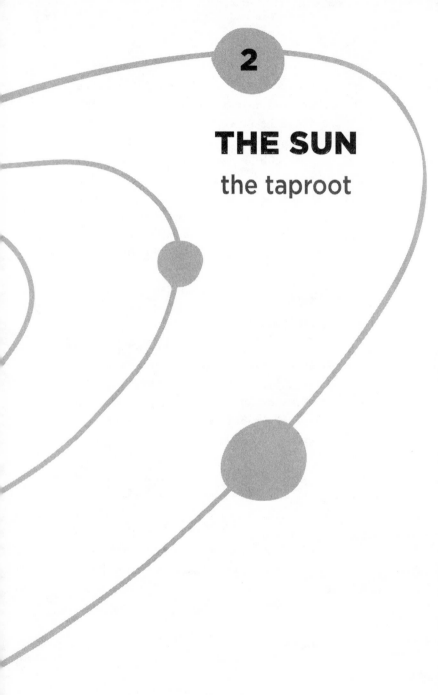

2

THE SUN
the taproot

The Sun represents the light through which all other parts of us shine. Our Sun sign describes our essence, our deepest energies and their expression in the world, the "I am . . ." of the astrological birth chart. Try this: start a sentence with "I am" and see what wants to flow next. What you answer will probably align in some important way with your Sun sign. The Sun sign is our most central self and the source of our most fundamental drives and expressions.

The astrology sign of our Sun speaks to one of our greatest karmic challenges: *will we rise to the most evolved version of ourselves, or will we let self-doubt cast us in the shadows or incite self-sabotage?*

THE MYTH OF APOLLO

In the old mythology, the god Apollo symbolizes the Sun. Apollo was the son of Zeus and Leto, born with a twin sister, Artemis. In one origin myth, Apollo was born to Leto, with Artemis's help, just after Leto had escaped from the giant serpent Python. Four days after his birth, Apollo exacted revenge on Python and claimed his shrine in Delphi.

Apollo grew up to be a god of light, music, and poetry, leader of the choir of muses. He was an embodiment of both physical beauty and virtuous morality—the bringer of inner light, whose ultimate message was to know thyself. He was known for his ability to think clearly and lead with reason.

Apollo defined self-knowledge as the goal and self-mastery as the "promised land"—the self as defined through goals and achievement.

TAPROOT

Plants can have either a fibrous root system—many roots of similar sizes—or a taproot, which grows a main root down into the soil with many small roots branching off. The archetype of the Sun is like the taproot to the degree that we develop our talents and gifts from top to bottom in a solid, responsible, conscientious way, with tributaries emerging to channel the nourishment of that light out to those around us. This new image takes this luminous energy down into the Earth and out toward other life-giving arteries. Taproots must receive energy from sunlight to grow strong, connect, and sustain, and they are fortified by anchoring deep into the Earth's body.

The symbol of the taproot turns us toward a quest for self-realization that paves the way to ennoble others in *their* divine light. The evolving possibility of the Sun as taproot is that each person becomes so bright that everyone around them is awakened to their own activation of light.

THE SUN IN THE SIGNS

The Sun in the chart relates to ego structure and sense of self. It represents the urge to *be* and to create, to be recognized and expressed. Its sign reflects the primary ways we identify ourselves and organize our multiple parts into a cohesive personality.

Sun in Aries

When you think of Sun in Aries, think of the caveman, devoted to fending off wild beasts and finding food and shelter for his tribe. Think of Wonder Woman. Think of the Nike slogan: *just do it*. Aries Sun people tend to be high energy, fiery, direct, and forceful. They are natural initiators who are good at making things happen. The flip side of this powerhouse sign can be impulsivity, ego-centeredness, or immaturity.

PRIMITIVE When you get caught up in the most primitive expression of Aries Sun, you're all about *me-me-me-me-me-me-me*. If anyone in your sphere forgets how very important you are, even for a second, they can expect to be reminded—and not in a shy or understated way. What you want is what *everybody* should want—to be totally *into you*. You know exactly how you want things to go, and if you don't get your way, someone's going to get punished.

ADAPTIVE You are courageous and protective of others. You willingly take a stand and fight for fairness, especially when people are being bullied or oppressed in any way. You make it a point to use your considerable strength and confidence to uplift those who most need a hand.

EVOLVING Your leadership is in service of social justice and causes that include all people, especially those who are most disenfranchised. Whatever talents or gifts you have been endowed with, you offer to those whose needs are greater than yours. Your ego strengths are there to serve the collective. You ask, often, with your trademark fiery energy and drive, wherever you go: *how can I can be most effective in delivering my gifts?*

Mara, whose Sun is in Aries, runs her ranch at night; by day, she runs a city newspaper. In both realms, she uses her pioneering spirit in service of her community. Nothing stands in her way of bringing the news to the people, fresh and bold, and making sure the animals are fenced in at night.

Mara works constantly in service of the community, whether it be the community of people who read the paper or the community of animals she shepherds on the ranch.

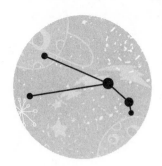

Sun in Taurus

Taurus Sun people are usually *yummy*: grounded, earthy, physical, calm, and beautiful in the same way rocks, mountains, fields, and valleys are beautiful. Liabilities of this Sun sign may include stubbornness, laziness, or grasping at material wealth or security.

PRIMITIVE   If your Sun is in Taurus and you're in your most unskillful place, you might be overheard saying, like a toddler in tantrum mode, "Mine! Mine! Mine! Give it to me! I need more!" Someone wants you to share? Out of the question!

Of course you're saying that—in this space, you believe that what you *have* is all of who you *are*. The more you have, the better your chances of being safe and okay in the world. You want it all, but you most definitely don't want to work for it, and nobody better ask you to lift a finger.

The less you need to do, the better. You feel it is only right for others, if they want you, to come to you and make you comfortable, feed you grapes, rub your feet, and arrange your cushions. Otherwise, they can take a hike.

ADAPTIVE   Your insecurities relax, taking some of your stubbornness with them. You are ready to share your resources, confident in your ability to conserve and grow the value of what you possess. Because you're no longer a screeching toddler who refuses to share, you have the space in your mind and heart to appreciate beauty, and you find joy in sharing your aesthetic sense with others. You begin to feel yourself as a rock that others can lean upon.

EVOLVING   As your sense of security grows, you can let your solidity and deep sense of continuity and responsibility be a calm and constant resource for others. Your sense of being a rock of support deepens; not only can you be a sturdy place of rest for those who need one, you are also capable of embracing and restoring anyone who has come to you to regroup. You realize that you most feel your value not in what you cling to but in what you give away.

Sun in Gemini

Gemini Sun people are usually talkative, intelligent, and clever. They have remarkable physical and mental dexterity and thrive on being connected with others through verbal communication. In their more Primitive modes, they can get caught up in unimportant details or be gossipy, spacey, or distracted.

PRIMITIVE   "Blah, blah, blah, blah! Did you see that video about . . . ? Did you know this arcane fact about . . . ? Don't get distracted—listen to my blah, blah, blah, because I need to just say whatever comes to my mind, and you need to listen with rapt attention!"

With your Sun in Gemini, at your least skillful, you pass on information whether or not it's correct. You like to be a gossip mill, spreading rumors—to have the gift of gab just to work your jaws. When you can't find an appropriately attentive listener, you feel lonesome and panicky, and you just might start making your stories more interesting through embellishment and confabulation in order to get someone to lend you their ear.

ADAPTIVE As you attain a more mature expression of Gemini Sun, you see that the actual content of conversation matters. You begin to notice your own skill with communication and use it to help other people connect. You find that people needing opportunities and possibilities begin to come to you for support, and you refine your communication skills so you can effectively share truthful information and knowledge. Everything you learn, you pass on to others, but you grow more sensitive to awaiting the right time and place for this transmission.

EVOLVING Your words themselves are deeds. You speak only from a sacred understanding that every word is a living being. Your sentences are sacraments for others to know their worth and their beloved nature on this Earth. You dedicate yourself to a deep understanding of higher wisdom and philosophy; in turn, you teach from a place of utter humility. You understand that you are always at the beginning of your own spiritual education.

One of the cleverest people I know, Kim has her Sun in Gemini. She is the network connection for every resource and person you'd ever want to know. When she's not gabbing on the phone helping everybody get connected, she's reading up on the latest trends and cultural offerings to make sure she always has relevant information to give out.

Sun in Cancer

Cancer Sun people tend to be empathic and deeply emotional nurturers. They may also be oversensitive, clingy, or needy.

PRIMITIVE   As a Cancer Sun, you deeply desire to nurture others—but when you're unskillful about it, you use this super-power to bind others to you as emotional hostages. You mother others to get them to be dependent on you. Any perceived crit-icism, judgment, or exclusion makes you lash out, disappear, or retaliate. If others don't mind-read your needs, you turn to manipulative, unreasonable emotional blackmail.

ADAPTIVE   Emerging from your watery den of emotional reactivity, you notice that there are other people out there, and you can sense their emotional vulnerability. You begin to use that ability to take care of them. You see that vulnerability is your superpower and that tending to others is exactly the key to your becoming more resilient and purposeful in your own life. Your ways of loving always prioritize others' sensitiv-ity, and you begin to receive great satisfaction from knowing others are well cared for.

EVOLVING   Your reservoir of feeling is so deep and vast that anyone in your presence will sense their capacity for feeling magnified in all kinds of ways. In yourself and others, you safe-guard the great Mother Goddess and all her extraordinary ways of nurturing the planet. You come to see how the emotional ecosystem and the actual ecosystems of nature work in concert on behalf of the evolution of humanity and the planet. You stand as the reflection, support, and guardian of human and natural ecosystems.

Sun in Leo

Leo Sun people tend to be creative, loving, and openhearted. They are often gifted in some way as performers or presenters. They can also be self-centered and needful of a great deal of approbation and attention.

PRIMITIVE   Your Sun in Leo means you are the star at all times. You expect to be bowed to, elevated, and promoted and to have an endlessly attentive entourage who will listen to your stories and shower you with compliments. You have nothing to offer to those who do not adore you.

ADAPTIVE   You find that entertaining others brings you to a sense of your own capacity for joy and that, in your presence, others can touch into their own childlike enthusiasm and exuberance. You realize that the greatest privilege of being alive is to play, and you begin to want to share that joy with others.

EVOLVING   Your heart becomes a searchlight for others' magnificence. All your gifts and talents are here for you to rise within your own aperture for loving. Your purpose is to awaken love wherever you are and to be an avatar of unconditional love and acceptance.

Satcha, whose Sun is in Leo, was raised in a privileged family and lacked for nothing. She was the youngest of four children and the only girl. She was doted on from day one and had a silver spoon in her mouth in terms of getting any material thing she wanted.

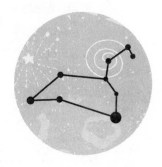

With her Sun in Leo, she grew up expecting lights to shine on her and to be adored and admired by family and friends alike. She focused highly on her personal appearance and her attractiveness at the expense of deeper exploration. She could enter a room and take all the attention onto herself, and she delighted in that. During her junior high and high school years, she became quite a competent artistic performer. She was addicted to the accolades that came from performing and being the star, so she decided to pursue a career in entertainment to fulfill her ultimate narcissistic dream of being famous.

Luckily for her, she had a string of self-absorbed boyfriends who taught her—through great heartache—that being central doesn't always equal being loved. At one point, she gained an incredible amount of weight due to hormonal imbalances and the stress of trying to love people who cheated on and lied to her. This led her into a deep period of introspection and a reconsideration of her values.

Through this year of a "dark night of the soul," she realized that the acting career she had so craved was also a place of constant rejection and humiliation. At this point, she met some key people who introduced her to the idea of her being a spiritual teacher. She spent the next several years studying spiritual disciplines and learning to love herself by inner standards instead of outer measures.

Satcha is now a highly regarded spiritual teacher whose entire teaching is based on self-acceptance and universal love. Her light is palpable from miles away because she is living the ultimate expression of Leo Sun: to inspire and encourage everyone to open their hearts.

Sun in Virgo

Virgo Sun people tend to be responsible, disciplined, and organized. They know there is a right way and a wrong way to do things, and they will ground down into the work required to make sure things are done right. They also have a great capacity for service and for finding the balance needed to integrate their bodies, minds, and spirits in service where it is needed. Virgo Sun people can tip into states of being perfectionistic, persnickety, and nitpicky and of being overly generous with unwanted advice.

PRIMITIVE   In your Primitive Virgo Sun, you live in fear of being judged, so you are sure to judge others first. Imperfection offends you, and you don't hesitate to offer corrections liberally to others. You serve, but you do so in order to earn approval. In fact, you'll make yourself sick from martyrdom, if necessary, just to get others' attention.

ADAPTIVE   You are driven by the need to engage in acts of kindness and helpfulness. You come to want others to realize that you are very specifically looking for ways to improve your well-being, and you begin to refine your organizing strategies. You focus on self-development, coming to know that walking your talk as a physically, mentally, and spiritually healthy person is the best way to encourage others in their own development.

EVOLVING   All of your perceptive techniques are used to generate an organizational experience of divine compassion and acceptance. Your service emanates from a sense of being a conduit for spiritual harmony and wisdom. You exemplify mind-body-spirit amalgamation. Through you, others experience imperfection as the pathway to enlightenment.

Sun in Libra

Libra Sun people are committed to balance, social harmony, and justice. They tend to be talkative, engaging, and beautiful in a symmetrical, classic way. Unskillful Libra expression can show up as shallowness—whether as being overly focused on how they are seen by others or as having an obsession with beauty that overshadows other important matters.

PRIMITIVE   A Primitive Libra expression means pretending to care about others only as a way of being special. You focus mainly on your own appearance: What do others think of you? How are you coming off? Do you look good? You avoid going deep at any cost because that deep dive might reveal some ugliness.

ADAPTIVE   You have developed an extraordinary skill for bringing others out of their shells. You are a quintessential question-asker and have tremendous compassion. When others are with you, they feel themselves as the center of your glowing attention. You feel joined with them in that central attention, and you blossom.

EVOLVING   All your social antennae and unique aesthetic gifts go toward raising the bar for social harmony. Through you, others come to recognize that balance and peace are created when we agree and share our perspective with "Yes, and . . . ," instead of countering and arguing with "Yes, but . . . ." Your mediation skills are unsurpassed because you willingly become invisible so that core truths that seem disparate can find their uniting principle.

Sun in Scorpio

People with Scorpio Sun tend to have enormous depth, intensity, and courage in truth telling; they want to live directly in the sexy beating heart of things. They are not afraid to transform the current reality, even when there is a price to pay for that transformation. Scorpio Sun people are often secretive and guarded, and their tremendous depth and deep, watery energy can sometimes translate to destructive force.

PRIMITIVE A Primitive Scorpio Sun expression can look like an addiction to intensity as a source of power. If you are living this out, you are fueled by the dark side, and you bring others down with you at any opportunity. Lust, envy, and greed propel you to constantly vie for power so that no one can ever be superior to you. You live to dominate because you cannot tolerate being submissive.

ADAPTIVE Your laser-like focus and devotion help others galvanize their powers of concentration. You use your emotional fuel to help other people solve problems and transform seemingly impenetrable situations. Your sexual energy is a source of vitality for yourself and others and is tied to generative creativity instead of egoistic debauchery.

EVOLVING You are the cosmic reboot. When others are feeling absolutely defeated, you are the power source of rebirth—emotionally, intellectually, and physically. Power pours through you; you are a sort of battery that energizes others to increase their levels of social dedication and innovation. You help yourself and others metabolize the dark forces into a compost for magic, wizardry, and clairvoyance.

Sun in Sagittarius

Sagittarius Sun people tend to be adventurous, knowledge-able seekers. They are expansive social connectors who thrive in the pursuit of higher learning and truth—and they love to party. In less skillful moments, they can come across as self-aggrandizing, bossy know-it-alls.

PRIMITIVE   As a Sagittarius Sun in its Primitive expression, you expect others to believe whatever you say, even if you're making it up—but not to worry, if you said it, it *must* be true. You are an expert at bragging, as well as at overpromising and underdelivering. You consider yourself the life of the party, and no one should even consider partying without you.

ADAPTIVE   You begin to seek the truest motivations—those that are about service, uncovering and sharing important truths, and expanding your knowledge. What knowledge you are able to glean, you freely use to enhance your experience. Your travels and social liaisons with others are springboards for your edification, and you hope to inspire others to expand their horizons. You continue your quest despite knowing you will never reach the destination of your own mastery.

EVOLVING   Your contagious joy in learning is fodder for all others to pursue their noble truths. You know there are a thousand ways to kneel and pray; the most important thing is for each person to find the beliefs that nourish them and move them to a higher appreciation of their essence. You are the bridge between people's doubts and their secure understanding of their part in the greater whole.

Sun in Capricorn

Capricorn Sun people tend to be industrious, responsible, action oriented, and good at thinking ahead. They thrive on achievement and love hard work—and on receiving appreciation for these qualities and the endeavors they fuel. In their less skillful expressions, they can be stressed-out overachievers, overly ambitious and overly needful of compliments.

PRIMITIVE You do what you do only so others will be impressed. You're the busiest person you know, and you stay that way all the time. You also make sure everyone else knows how very busy you are, so they'll recognize your importance and the wealth of knowledge you bring to the table. You are ambitious for the sake of reaching the top, even though you have no clue why you're scrambling toward it. The best thing anyone can do is talk about you as one of the supreme experts in your field.

ADAPTIVE You use your considerable competencies to support and uplift other people's experience of their proficiencies. You come to recognize that your ability to scale ideas into actionable items can help others achieve their greatest dreams; this gives you enormous joy and satisfaction. You begin to give others your all, so that all people can come to know their worth.

EVOLVING You align with a duty to ensure that all beings know they have an unquestionably vital role in the evolution of human consciousness. You are the mountain upon which every person can rest, regroup, and return to a sense of purpose. It makes no difference what others think of you, but it matters greatly that you leave a legacy of value on this Earth—a value determined not by material compensation or rating but by leaving the planet a better place than you found it.

Sun in Aquarius

An Aquarius Sun person is naturally community minded. They tend to have big, overarching ideas about how the world could be and how we can all work together to realize those positive visions. They are highly intuitive and are good at thinking abstractly and creatively. Some liabilities of Aquarius Sun: they can be *too* abstract and difficult to tether to earthly limitations; they can be aloof, arrogant, and unpersonable—sometimes even rude and cold, especially when others fail to keep up with the fast-moving train of their visionary ideas.

PRIMITIVE　As an Aquarius Sun, you know *everything*. Why should anyone else even bother to speak? You are cold and indifferent to others because they only exist as a cog in your greater wheel of ideas. It's not just that you are snobbish and aloof; it's also that you actually think human beings are a low expression of creation.

ADAPTIVE　Your awakening skills are in service of bringing humanity together for the greater good. Your bigger-picture awareness allows others to find their seat at the table and to feel welcomed and inspired. Your lightning intuition is an offering for others to tap into what they know to be true and to bring it out through creative expression.

EVOLVING　You realize that you have come to this plane of existence to weave a tapestry of all colors. Around you, all will be encouraged to see the brilliance and hue of every human being. You dissolve into the fabric of others' enlightened perspectives and help knit together the broken pieces of all humanity, recognizing that each colorful swath is as important as the whole.

Sun in Pisces

Pisces Sun people tend to be exquisitely sensitive, creative, and emotionally vulnerable. They are strongly tuned in to the worlds of dreams and to the oceanic realm where all things merge into one consciousness. Because they can so easily merge with the feeling states of others, they have amazing gifts of compassion and empathy. In their less skillful expressions, Pisces Sun people respond to the pain and intensity of being strongly tuned in to the universal consciousness by clicking into victim thinking, addiction, and escapism.

PRIMITIVE In your least skillful place, you as Pisces Sun can come to think of yourself mostly as a victim of your circumstances and of other people. You think that everything in life just happens to you, and you bear no responsibility, nor do you have any power. Why shouldn't you just escape and be numbed out? Pass the bottle; pass the pills! You go into the addictive, escapist place because reality is just too hard and totally not worthwhile. If that doesn't work, you just make everyone else miserable with a lot of whining and wanking.

ADAPTIVE You begin to recognize how your incredible sensitivity can act as a vessel for enlarging and growing your creative imagination. Through asking for and receiving emotional and physical support, you feel empowered to be as expressed as you can possibly be. You can then help others acknowledge their vulnerability and tenderness in ways that become critical strengths of their characters. You apply your ancestral DNA of softness and kindness to help others find their confidence in everything they do.

EVOLVING   You are a wave of consciousness that reminds others that they are sparks of divine creation and partners with the Creative itself. In the vast container of who you are, the seas of others' own undivided nature become apparent, and the exquisite interplay of the muses and their creations are woven together.

Tom has a Pisces Sun. He is a dream weaver who literally leads dream workshops all over the world. With his Sun in Pisces, he can instantly drop into an enormous pool of compassion. He sees into the deepest, most sensitive feelings of others; he makes others feel as if—for the first time—all their feelings are welcome. Tom has built a life around creating possibilities for other people's dreams. He lives near the ocean and consistently renews himself there, where he swims with his friends the sharks and plays with families of dolphins.

Practices for the Sun • • • • • • • • • •

Dive In

Based on your Primitive Sun sign description, write, without any censorship, a list of ten ways you operate from this level in your life. Observe that this lower application of your Sun sign is a collective programming of which you are unwittingly a part.

Now, take those same ten qualities of under-resourced behavior and turn them into five qualities that you would like to install inside yourself. Come up with a power list and a power pose for fully inhabiting these new qualities. For example:

> Sun in Aries: bold, protective, pioneering, considerate, tender
>
> Now, strike a physical pose that somehow conveys this to you and shines it out for others. Take a picture of yourself in your new pose and share it with a friend.
>
> Or:
>
> Write a letter to your inner child who acts in primitive ways because your needs weren't being met. What would you like to say to that inner child now? How would you care for and love them? How can you support them in moving out of Primitive strategies into more mature ways of being?

Reach Out

Think of two stories from your life that bring up regrets about how you have used your Sun energy.

Write a summary of those two stories and view them from an objective distance. This will help you see which hurt parts of you were running the show.

Then, get together with a loved one or friend. Discuss with them what you are learning about yourself and others when you act out of a less-than-developed Sun place. Invite them to do this same exercise so that it's a dialogue, not a monologue.

Risk It

Pick one of the Evolving sentences from your Sun sign.

Commit to doing an act of creation that reflects the absolute intention of that Evolved Sun expression.

Make something happen that demonstrates your commitment to this Evolved place of your Sun.

Write down the results of this action and why it is important to the essence of who you are.

Reflect

With the visual talisman of the taproot or a place in nature, spend ten minutes reflecting on the highest vibration of your Sun sign expression.

Ask to be guided by the physical planet (the Sun) in your maturation as a cosmic citizen.

When you are done, write a poem about the messages given to you. I've provided an example to help inspire and encourage your expression. When I did this Reflection practice, this is what came to me through my Aquarius Sun:

> No one sounds the same if they are truly themselves
> The words form differently in every mind and mouth
> They play in the air with different rhythms and tempos
> Our worlds are constructed by narratives
> A string of words influences entire populations
> We need to break out
> linked in the embrace of each other's
> truth telling

Wait for no one to begin
Share your stumbling trembling efforts
We will grow strong from the rising of our words

Talking Circle Questions

Gather with one or more people who have read this chapter. As a group, choose a talking piece.* Have each person answer the following questions, one at a time. Make sure there is no cross-talk or side-talk; this is a time for completely undistracted, uninterrupted sharing. Before beginning, agree to keep what is said in the circle confidential, to listen deeply, to speak without rehearsing, and to be aware of time so that all have a chance to answer each question in the time available.

1. Name a time when you exhibited the lowest Primitive vibration of your Sun sign. How did it affect you? How did it impact others?

2. Name a situation in which you repeatedly used your Adaptive Sun sign traits. What results did you achieve?

3. Talk about what it would mean to you or those around you if you were able to sustain the Evolving Sun sign traits for even 20 percent of each day.

4. Put each person in the circle on the "hot seat" and have the others in the circle, one by one, name qualities of that person's intrinsic radiance.

---

* A talking piece is an object used to signify that the holder of the piece can speak without interruption. It can be a stone, stick, set of beads, or crystal, or even a less significant object like a pen or stuffed toy. As long as one person in the circle is holding the talking piece, it is their turn to speak; they should pass the talking piece only when they have fully finished responding to the question.

I live to feel. I feel to live.

ANONYMOUS

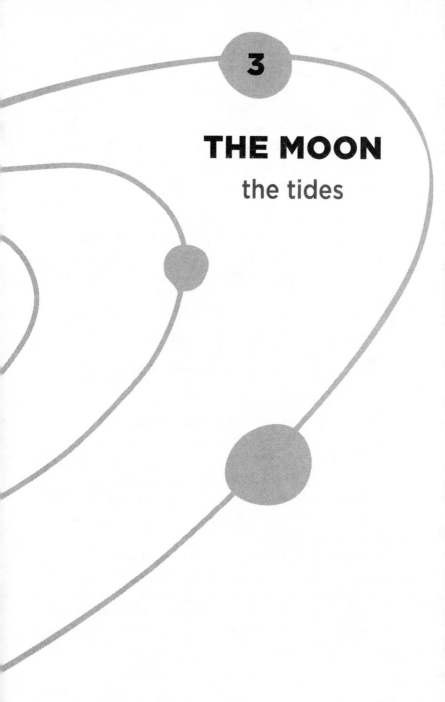

THE MOON
the tides

The moon represents our nonnegotiable emotional needs and the ways in which we organize ourselves for emotional fulfillment. Where the Sun represents "I am," the Moon represents "I need." It represents the emotional, instinctive, responsive part of the self; the unconscious; the part of the self that mothers and nurtures others. It also conveys the nature of our relationships with our own mothers.

This is perhaps the most crucial part of understanding one's own psyche and realizing the true needs of those close to us. When we fully inhabit the skillful potentials of our lunar natures, we can swiftly and competently meet our own needs and serve the needs of others with great boundaries and empathy.

Modern culture has emphasized solar outer achievements, often at the expense of emotional authenticity. The Moon archetype teaches us that without fidelity to our innermost needs, we become decorated shells—hollow and empty.

THE MYTH OF THE TRIPLE GODDESS

The traditional myth of the astrological Moon is the triple goddess: the Maiden, the Mother, and the Crone. Each is symbolic of a separate stage in the female life cycle that corresponds to a phase of the Moon. Each rules one of the realms of Earth, the underworld, and the heavens, and each cycles through the life span in a predictable way.

While this depiction is helpful in understanding a life cycle of the feminine in standard terms, it falls short of representing the nonlinear experience of feeling. The archetypal Maiden is of a certain age and external appearance, as are the Mother and the Crone, and each archetype is associated with its own societally driven expectations.

Just like the light of the Moon in all its phases, we are cyclical—and yet, in the emerging mythology, we take a quantum leap into formless possibility. Sometimes we are eleven years old and feel like ancient elders; sometimes we are sixty and internally romping like a child. Shifting the mythology around the astrological Moon allows us to reimagine and reinvent ourselves without the constraints of age or time.

THE TIDES

Nature gives us the perfect metaphor for our emotional selves in the glorious shifting of the tides. Tides go very low and very high; sometimes their shifting is almost imperceptible, but they never stop changing.

To fully embrace our lunar capacities, we need to become like the shore—to receive the comings and goings of emotions as signals, not finalities. When we learn to ride with the tides, we can enjoy the variety and the unique perspective each emotional state offers us.

We also realize that we cannot control the occurrence of emotion and that there is beauty both in the extremes of emotion and in the temperate. Paying attention to the continuity of certain feelings allows us to know, from the inside out, what matters to us most.

There is no stopping the movement of the tides. The worst thing we can do to ourselves is try to block the flow and rationalize our way out of a deep feeling. Although it's possible to separate our emotional selves from our relationships and our actions, doing so deprives the world of the fullness of who we are and creates massive internal stress. Emotions convey vital information to us about how to be and what to do. Integrating that information into our daily lives is most possible when we know and accept our emotional selves.

Feelings want shores to land on and to be held and cared for. When we are unskillful in our emotional expression, we create emotional floods and tsunamis—and sometimes even droughts through stonewalling or shutdown. Vulnerability is a superpower; cultivating the ability to trust and reveal ourselves to vetted confidants is key to emotional health.

When we know what we feel and can share those feelings with precision (a skill psychologists call *emotional granularity*), we become highly responsible and effective in relationships. Expressing our emotional tides does not ensure that we get our relational needs met because those needs are always a negotiation between ourselves and others; however, when we let our emotional tides roll in and out with grace, we honor our own emotional needs. In doing so, we can do a great deal to meet those needs in ourselves, even when others in our lives cannot meet them.

THE MOON IN THE SIGNS

Understanding the sign placement of our Moon helps us feel connected to our essential natures and to the greater rhythms of life. Use what you learn in this chapter to better understand your own internal emotional nature and to begin to find healthy, creative outlets for sharing it with others.

To balance the energy of your Moon sign, it often helps to "work" its opposite. I'll mention this strategy in the description of each sign.

Moon in Aries

People with this placement usually are emotionally demonstrative. They want others to know how they're feeling and will express emotions with strength and directness. They also want to be the most emotionally important person in the room at any given time!

PRIMITIVE   The Primitive expression of Moon in Aries says to others that they don't really exist except to mirror you. "Enough about you; have you noticed how big and strong and bold and great I am?" When you're mad or sad or afraid or happy or whatever emotion you are, everyone had better pay attention—and it doesn't matter who gets hurt or obscured by your big expression. You readily fly off the handle when you are angry. Anyone who says "no" to whatever your emotions inspire you to want is in the way; they should step off and let you have your moment, and then another moment, and then another one after that.

The most important thing is that *you* get *your* emotional needs met; once that happens, *maybe* others can have needs and voice them, but it won't be long before it's time for everyone to attend to *your* needs some more.

ADAPTIVE   As Aries Moon finds a more skillful expression, you actively exercise your need to be assertive, protective, and straightforward in your requests. You come to be able to hear "no" with maturity. Rather than complaining about all that's causing you to have uncomfortable feelings, you begin to learn to make calm requests for things to change.

You take up a daily, vigorous exercise program to help you lengthen your short fuse. You actively learn appropriate ways to express anger that don't harm others or yourself. You begin to consider others' needs, as well as your own, and to respect the opinions and sensitivities of others. The part of you that loves to lecture makes way for the one who is willing to listen.

The opposite of Aries energy in the chart is Libra—balancing, seeking harmony and beauty. You can balance an Aries Moon by engaging in practices based on organizing and beautifying the spaces in which you live and work and by consciously trying to value the feelings and thoughts of others as much as you do your own.

EVOLVING In your most skillful Aries Moon expression, you come to see tenderness as a hallmark of courage. You stand up for others by expressing your emotional support as often and as gracefully as possible. You take impeccable care of your body and use your considerable emotional energy to mentor others in their own self-confidence. Through disciplined practices of self-awareness, calming, and centering, you come to be able to hear feedback with curiosity and humility. In any exchange with another person, you earnestly want to know what they are feeling and to connect with true understanding.

Moon in Taurus

Taurus Moon people have the potential to be emotionally steady and reliable. They are sensual and sensuous; most love to cuddle and to feel surrounded by earthy beauty. If their deep need for physical and material security seems threatened, a hoarding, stubborn side of Taurus Moon can be unleashed.

PRIMITIVE You won't let go. You will hold on until your fingers bleed. Stuck, unable to budge, you are mired in stinginess and the need for more, more, more. You feel that being stingy is actually virtuous. You bury yourself in pleasures, feeling righteously deserving, but they are never enough, and you never want to share. You cannot get touched and held enough, but that doesn't stop you from holding everyone around you responsible for touching you as often as possible. Underneath your neediness is a constant fear of abandonment and rejection.

ADAPTIVE You use your sturdy, reliable emotional self to buoy others when they feel sidetracked or lost. You feel the pleasure of being the rock for yourself and others to lean on to find peace and equanimity. In chaotic times, you are able to stay centered, and you find you can also hold the center for others. You use everything in moderation and feel utterly contented. Your body is your temple, and you feel sensually in touch with yourself and with nature.

The opposite of Taurus energy in the chart is Scorpio. As you lean into the energy of depth and transformation, you can take more risks in your relationships or dive into creative projects—anything that nudges you out of your comfort zone and into new ways of thinking and being.

EVOLVING In this iteration, you work to release your concerns around material security in favor of being grateful for everything you have. You employ strategies for taking excellent care of all your things and yourself. You know yourself to be a solid stand for the emotional needs of others. You use your exceptional skills of sensual attunement to help others get in touch with the beauty and majesty of their bodies at any shape or size. You are exceedingly generous because you understand the temporary nature of all things. You also understand that your freest happiness is to share what you can with others.

In his early life, teenager Brett, a Taurus Moon, was known for his stubbornness. When he wanted something and had strong feelings about it, he would dig down deep and hang on hard. He would never turn on anyone in anger; he would never yell at anyone or have

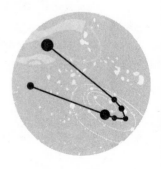

any kind of emotional outburst. In fact, his mom can barely remember him crying or shouting with emotion at all once he was out of his toddler phase. Instead, when he had big feelings, he would turn inward. His face would turn red; his stubborn determination would be written all over his face and body.

Brett's older sister tells a story about him wanting to be let into her room to hang out with her and a friend. When she refused, he sat right next to her door, emptied the family's sizable change bucket onto the hall floor, and loudly counted change for over an hour. This kind of endurance and perseverance was once a hallmark of Brett's strategy for trying to get his emotional needs met.

Over time, and with maturation and support, Brett began to rethink this strategy, seeing that it was causing people to avoid him more, rather than bringing them closer. And what he wanted most was to be close and comfortable with other people. He woke up the Scorpio energy in his chart by joining an after-school group where he could talk about his feelings in a safe space and where he got to push himself out of his comfort zone by learning to sing in front of an audience. He fed the earthy, materialistic side of Taurus Moon by doing more artistic projects; he was especially good at origami and making paper airplanes. In characteristic Earth-bound Taurus style, he even started to make beautiful dense spheres out of dirt (a Japanese art form called *dorodango*), spending hours sifting dirt and packing and polishing it into a glistening sphere about the size of a billiard ball.

As he began to tend his own feelings and to dive into self-exploration, other people were drawn to him. From what once looked to others like emotional shutdown began to emanate a stability, calm, and serenity that attracted everyone to him and made others love being in his company.

Moon in Gemini

Gemini Moon people love to talk and to be immersed in the world of thought and the power of the mind. They are emotionally fed by conversation and through the power of words and ideas. They are especially prone to sliding into a love affair with the Internet and may use its infinite realm of ideas as a distraction from unmet needs around feelings. When unskillful, they can be scattered and distractible and seem cold, supplanting the warmth of emotional connectivity with words, words, and more words—abstractions that can distract from the true heart of feeling connected.

PRIMITIVE Lost in your scattered thoughts, you talk incessantly without connecting. You keep distracting yourself to avoid feeling anything, and you use words as weapons.

ADAPTIVE You communicate your true needs with patience and clarity. You cultivate your listening skills so that you can take in other people's points of view, and you start to feel eager to respond to their needs. You are able to focus your thoughts and share them with poise and compassion.

You begin to expand your tolerance for meeting others in their emotional depths by diving fully into important relationships or taking on new endeavors that push you into new emotional territory. You may lean toward Gemini's fiery, adventurous, bold opposite, Sagittarius, to balance the energy of this placement, breaking out of airy patterns of thought and abstraction into physical doing and risking.

EVOLVING   You are able to use your ability to be objective and thoughtful about emotions in order to provide support and perspective to others. You are able to link your needs to the highest good and to speak articulately about all possible positive outcomes in any conflict.

Moon in Cancer

People with their Moon in Cancer are most emotionally fed by nurturing and caring for others and by being nurtured and cared for with tenderness and total acceptance. They have incredible mothering instincts, and they empathize easily. When their need for care and nurturance is not met, they can become clingy or lash out in frustration. Cancer Moon people may struggle with emotional reactivity and be easily overwhelmed by feeling.

In astrological wisdom, because Cancer is ruled by the Moon, this placement can intensify the feeling focus of both the planet and the sign, combining two energies that push in the same direction rather than balancing one another out.

PRIMITIVE   At its most immature and unskillful, your Cancer Moon throws a clingy fit if you have to do anything but be a baby in your mommy's arms, forever and ever, suckling away blissfully at her bountiful and nourishing breast. You would really rather not have to take care of yourself. When others expect you to do so, they learn quickly that whining is your favorite indoor sport.

You like comforting and nurturing others, but if they hurt you in any way, you withdraw your care from beneath them as quickly as a prankster pulls a chair out from beneath a person in the midst of sitting down. *Bam!* Too bad for them. They should have known better than to neglect or anger you.

ADAPTIVE You decide to nurture yourself with more intention, and you begin to nurture others from a place of fullness. Your vulnerability becomes a source of strength and motivates you to build your inner resources and emotional confidence. You know how to name all your feelings and find just the right ways to express them.

You explore the energies of Cancer's opposite, Capricorn—its sense of order, structure, solidity, and predictability. Perhaps you are a parent who develops a behavior and chore chart system with reward stickers; perhaps in your partner relationship, you implement a structured way of checking in, stating each person's needs, and planning ways to fulfill them; perhaps, in general, you become more disciplined around the ways you nurture others and yourself.

EVOLVING Through enlightened self-care, you reach divine heights where you can channel universal Mother energy to all those around you. Your selfless generosity contributes to everyone's feelings of safety and caring. Each day, you feel drawn to tend to the hurts of others in a structured and loving way.

Yasmin's Cancer Moon has made her feel as though she's afloat in a sea of feeling, vulnerable to being washed under by every swell that comes along. She has so much love inside of her and such a strong urge to use it to nurture others; but once she gets really close to someone, she fears overwhelming them with all her care and attention. This fear is merited, as it comes from repeated experiences of having people push her away because they can't handle the strength of her nurturing superpowers. Her fear of "being *too much*" in relationship has been realized more than once, and this has sent her into a painful tailspin every time.

She decided to spend at least a full year actively not looking for a partner (this took extreme willpower, as she was also feeling the Cancer Moon longing to become a mother). She turned her nurturing superpowers on herself and practiced fulfilling her own emotional needs. She felt intense loneliness and longing but had the discipline to stick with her commitment to be unpartnered.

When she was finally ready, a perfect person appeared—one who was willing to support her in her wobbly first steps back into relationship with new self-awareness; one who didn't spook easily when she fell back into old Primitive habits (which enabled her to course-correct and show up again in Adaptive and Evolving ways).

Moon in Leo

Moon in Leo people are deeply nourished by big emotions. They tend to be passionate, demonstrative, childlike, and open-hearted, and they readily express emotion through the creative arts. When they can't feed their need for emotional expression or if others don't seem to adequately appreciate their emotional fireworks, they can become greedy for attention and hungry for drama.

PRIMITIVE If your Leo Moon plays out in its most primitive form, you insist that others worship and adore you, despite your difficulty with ever really taking in that love. No matter how much adoration you receive, you want more—and more often. You are childish and refuse to grow up, and you expect those who love you to also love your drama.

ADAPTIVE   You begin to let your openheartedness shine high-wattage affection on others. People feel joyful in your company because you raise the bar for wonder and play. You lean into Leo's opposite, Aquarius, by sharing your gifts of powerful emotion and expressiveness across your community whenever you can, as well as by being a beacon of love who makes collaboration, cooperation, and visionary social change irresistibly interesting and exciting.

EVOLVING   Wherever you go, your supreme love of heartfelt self-expression is contagious and inviting. Where people feel unlovable, you shine your enormous light on their essence and affirm their unique expressions.

Moon in Virgo

Virgo Moon people are emotionally nourished by being of service. In Evolving iteration, this placement is a win-win in terms of satisfying the self, while also supporting the collective. Those with Moon in Virgo thrive in the quest to merge mind, body, and spirit; to work hard; and to be a support to others.

In its more Primitive state, the perfectionistic need to categorize and organize can smash the Virgo Moon into a paralyzing state of self-criticism. This state can easily translate to Virgo Moon people projecting their perfectionism on others.

PRIMITIVE   In your Primitive place, your Virgo Moon brings you to eviscerating self-criticism, where you can see flaws in every part of yourself. Consumed by details you feel unequipped to handle, you reject any attempts made by others to bring you out of your funk. You wish they wouldn't even try. There's no forgiving your inadequacy. You're like a cat clawing your way out of a tangle of blankets, and anyone who gets in there with you will be scratched mercilessly. It's all right, as you prefer to suffer alone.

ADAPTIVE You begin to feel the satisfaction of serving others' needs, even when you don't feel all that great about yourself. You see how you can restore your own emotional well-being by looking around to see what others need, and you become expert at identifying ways to be helpful. You freely offer your meticulous understanding and feel capable of being there for anyone who needs someone to listen to every emotional detail—including yourself.

Virgo's opposite, Pisces, is as much about dissolving boundaries as Virgo is about drawing them. You might summon that energy through a spiritual practice that helps you feel into the unity of all. A new workout program that involves swimming might have a similar balancing effect.

EVOLVING Your highly developed consideration and specific eye for service can assist anyone in becoming more discerning and effective in their emotional expression. You work hard to transform minutiae into meaningful conversation, using small pearls of wisdom to make a gorgeous necklace.

Moon in Libra

Libra Moon people are emotionally fed by being in relationships and by beauty and harmony. They feel most expressed when connecting with others, usually through talking; they feel especially satisfied emotionally when creating relationship harmony or resolving differences. Considering these needs and wants, it's not surprising that Libra Moon people often feel drawn toward psychotherapy as a career. An overinvestment in looking good and presenting to others well can be a downside for someone with Moon in Libra. People with this placement can also feel lost or worthless when not mirrored by other people.

PRIMITIVE When your Moon in Libra is immature and unskillful, you have no core without the other's reflection. If they are not happy, you feel as though you are nothing. You are lost without the other, and you cannot bear it when they don't respond to you. You can only feel your worth through your exterior presentation. If you don't look good, you are unlovable, and you feel as though shame is the skin you live in.

ADAPTIVE You are able to feel all sides of any situation, which makes you a fabulous mediator. You exist in a state of emotional balance, harmony, and beauty, and you take great care to keep your scales of emotion as even as possible. You listen for and draw out people's gifts.

Drawing on the qualities of Libra's opposite, Aries, in your emotional life helps you energize your more selfish parts, and in your situation, that's a good thing. You need that forward-thrusting energy to avoid the inertia and to focus on appearances that can undermine your emotional well-being. Vigorous physical activity helps balance a Libra Moon, as does having strategies and support for getting unstuck when decisions feel hard to make.

EVOLVING Your radiant temperance is a beacon inviting all people to feel their own emotional steadiness. When others are with you, they are instantly inspired into a field of reciprocity. You allow yourself to be exquisite without fancy embellishment.

With her Moon in Libra, Rachel has sometimes felt lost when she cannot positively impact others. In those times, she has struggled with a feeling of helplessness when she sees others doing things she feels are wrong and who then won't listen to her advice about how to better themselves. Over time, she has learned to sit with this discomfort and to be a shining example of emotional equanimity in her own right. She still often feels the sting of injustice but chooses not to act upon it, instead working out that discomfort by focusing on determined self-improvement and action.

Moon in Scorpio

Scorpio Moon people tend to be secretive, private, and emotionally deep and intense. Their feeling selves need extreme connections and states of being to feel satisfied. Where the shadow side of things goes unrecognized, their emotional needs cannot be met. There is enormous energy stored away in this placement; when it is not channeled skillfully, it can explode into self-hatred and a conviction that the person does not and cannot belong in this world.

PRIMITIVE At its most unskillful, your Scorpio Moon concocts stories about your being contemptible, unworthy, and dark. You hate yourself, and sometimes you believe that something is terribly wrong with you—even that you deserve to die. You feel your own intensity like a sword in your heart. You feel like cautioning others to stay away; you are poisonous and should never let anyone in far enough to suffer the consequences of exposure to that poison. You see evidence everywhere that you are unlovable, but you still feel that the right thing for you to do to those who have spurned you is to exact revenge.

ADAPTIVE   You begin to learn to transmute dark emotions swiftly, turning them into self-assertive motivation. You help others withstand their most difficult emotions and help them feel loved and accepted. You can attach to others passionately, knowing that all love ends one day in death. You embrace this as a reason to be even more present in your emotional connections to others.

You explore the opposing energies of Taurus, with their calming, grounded, earthy, cuddly sensuousness, to balance your intensity. Perhaps you take up gardening or beautifying your home; perhaps you seek out a wonderful bodyworker who can help you move heightened energies through your body in a way that releases the tensions of this placement; perhaps you make frequent dates to make slow, sensuous, calm love with your partner, appealing to the deep sexiness of Scorpio energies through a much more calming way of being that also reassures you that you are cared for, adored, and accepted just as you are.

EVOLVING   Your extraordinary capacity for depth is used to host others in their range of feeling and to teach them how to transform difficult states into strengths and creative possibilities. You are fearless in facing your own shadow. You realize that you are equipped to support the collective in working through negative projections and to come through those projections with renewed determination and incalculable emotional resiliency. You specialize in letting others know how much they matter, and you verbally and creatively share your insights and appreciations with laser-like focus and earnestness.

Alexandra has her Moon in Scorpio. She married young to an older man who was commanding, powerful, creative, and sexy. With Edward, Alexandra felt safe and protected. She knew she had found a great provider to have children with. In her family of origin, intense emotions were not acceptable, except in alcoholic bursts of inappropriate anger. She learned to hide her feelings deep inside and cover them up with a very accommodating persona.

Edward was a demonstrative and expressive partner who also struggled with anger, but that seemed somewhat normal to Alexandra. They had two beautiful children together, and Alexandra buried herself in her children's lives and her passions for horticulture and homeopathy. Over the course of ten years, Alexandra became more and more unhappy in the marriage, as Edward seemed to grow more and more temperamental. Eventually they decided to separate and to keep the children their main united focus through loving parenting.

Alexandra then met Shawn, the love of her life. This man was committed to knowing and expressing his emotions. He saw through Alexandra's reluctance to share her inner life. Through their intimate, intense courtship, Alexandra learned a new love language. She began to feel all the unfelt feelings of her life and to confide in Shawn about her fears and vulnerabilities. She no longer ran from her dark side but eagerly shared her discoveries with her love. She also realized, with regret, how much she had asked Edward to carry her dark side. Now she understood that in order to truly love, one must be willing to risk the vulnerability that leads to genuine connection.

Moon in Sagittarius

Sagittarius Moon people need adventure, higher learning, and being on the go in order to feel emotionally satisfied. They feel fed emotionally when teaching or guiding others. They want to experience the divine, and they enjoy diving into religious or philosophical studies or conversations. They thrive on new experiences and on ideas that expand the mind; they are great at telling entertaining stories and making others laugh.

When in an unskillful place, Sag Moon folks can find themselves unable to connect with others at a deep level. They are fed more by the broadness of experience than by the intimacy of relationship. Where they do not feel met in their aspirations and knowledge, they may just run—rationalizing that they aren't beloved in that relationship anyhow—rather than stay and struggle with feeling connected. They can feel fearful of being held back by those who are not willing to join in risking and seeking and can be harsh with others when they fear rejection.

PRIMITIVE   You feel a desire to escape all emotional attachments when in your Primitive expression of Sagittarius Moon because you might get smothered. You live from a place of fear of connecting because you don't believe anyone could love you as you really are. When in doubt of others' affection, you run far and fast. You can say really mean things if you feel backed into a corner.

ADAPTIVE   You learn to set people free with the exuberant humor and laughter that come naturally to you. You see meaning in everything and take nothing for granted. People come to you to hear the truth related thoughtfully.

Gemini, Sagittarius's opposing energy, breathes space and light into the fiery feeling states of Sagittarius Moon. You might find balance by stepping back from the singular, driving focus of Sag to expand your pursuit of learning in mind, body, and spirit.

EVOLVING   You see the divine in every interaction. Joy overrides all other feelings: the joy of being a free human being who sees the cup full—always full. People feel an incredible sense of expansiveness around you.

Moon in Capricorn

Capricorn Moon people need to feel as though everything is in order. Predictability, structure, and fulfilled responsibilities satisfy their emotional needs. This outlook extends to the way they appear to others, including their carefully vetted and well-thought-out outfits and the decor they create in their homes. The difficulties of this placement include a craving for completion and organization that is never satisfied, leading to restlessness and distraction, which stand in the way of relaxing into life as it is. There is also an overfocus on and an overidentification with appearances and a desperate need for external validation and approval. Deep feeling can be a tough call indeed for Capricorn Moon folks.

PRIMITIVE You live for praise, but you are never good enough. You compare yourself to others incessantly and feel like you will never achieve enough to be okay. You are cold to others when they do not demonstrate that they approve of you and all your choices. You live in an emotionally sterile bubble so that you can be in control of your losses.

ADAPTIVE You are a steward of emotion management. You feel everything deeply and allow others to know you need them. With you, people feel that their best features are held high and acknowledged. You are responsive to and responsible for mature conversations of mutual interest.

Opposite Capricorn in the astrological mandala is watery, deeply feeling Cancer. Steps to balance Capricorn Moon energy might include dedicating time every day to consciously entering a space of feeling. One Capricorn Moon person I know would start each day with "morning tears"—she would surf around on social media to find a video that made her cry with joy, grief, or other deep emotions. Focused intimacy work with a therapist or trusted guide or reading any of Brené Brown's wonderful books about vulnerability could help break through the natural remove of this Moon placement.

EVOLVING You can be counted on to be the lead in any life-changing emotional discussion about ethical and moral courage. Others feel so validated by you that they open up and learn great life lessons in your presence.

Moon in Aquarius

Aquarius Moon people are most emotionally fed through communitarian pursuits: gatherings of lots of people in some form or another (whether virtually or in real life) and conversations about visionary ideas and plans. They are comfortable embracing the many facets of the whole of existence and are most contented when they feel that everyone is taken care of and no one is being left out. However, it can be challenging for the Aquarius Moon person to drop into feeling—when they're stuck in that soup, they can no longer see the big picture, and that's disorienting and scary for this Moon placement.

PRIMITIVE In an unskillful Aquarius Moon place, you are impervious. No feelings happen inside you. You are all platitudes and rationalizations. You are better than everyone else, so why should you bother dealing with lowly emotions? It's up to you to dwell in the future and focus on the big picture—and conveniently, this spares you from any recognition that you might be less significant than you think.

ADAPTIVE You are a trustworthy, supportive, and wonderful friend who sees and loves all that others are. With you, others feel all their parts integrated into a lovable whole. When they are with you, they feel life as wide open, like an endless blue sky.

Working the opposite energy to Aquarius—Leo—means cultivating playfulness, joy, and direct experience, rather than an airy blizzard of ideas. The Aquarius Moon person might benefit from the physicality of intense exercise or from some form of expressive creative art. Deep one-on-one connection will help counter the spread-out communitarian focus of Aquarius Moon.

EVOLVING You provide a large enough emotional space for everyone's peculiarities to feel valued and included. The swath of acceptance people feel from you heals them to the core and helps them be more compassionate. People excel as equals around you.

Anthony Bourdain, the much-loved chef and author who committed suicide in 2018, had his Moon in Aquarius. I bring him in here not to caution Aquarius Moon people about suicide risk—the choice to take one's own life is never about a single factor in the birth chart—but because I see him as having so beautifully exemplified skillfulness with this placement.

While Bourdain often came across as a curse-word-heavy misanthrope, anyone who read his books or watched his television programs could see that he loved life, he loved people, and he wanted what was best for everyone and for the world. He was a visionary thinker and brilliant connector. His writings delved into deeply personal territory for the ultimate purpose of bringing people together in awakening—and in doing so, trying to realize a better situation for as many people as possible. He spoke out on behalf of women involved in the #MeToo movement and for immigrants who do the lion's share of work in America's restaurants.

Moon in Pisces

The person with Moon in Pisces is swimming in a sea of feeling, able to touch into this world and the next. Psychic abilities are not unusual in Pisces Moon people. They need to feel the oneness of everything—a oneness that is a dream rather than a nightmare. When expressed unskillfully, the person with this placement feels overwhelmed by emotion and unable to function; they feel victimized by people and circumstances. Sometimes, the only way to manage these feelings is to use drugs or alcohol or to completely check out.

PRIMITIVE You are a sniveling, snot-dripping mess. You cannot function because you are drowning in feelings. Others always hurt you, and everyone is out to get you. No one understands you, and you just cannot catch a break in life. You can't take it. You want out of here.

ADAPTIVE As you come to realize that you have the power to literally feel what others feel, you get that this is an amazing skill that can heal others. You cultivate your capacity to touch into the feeling states of others, and your empathy goes right to their center and warms their hearts. Through your artful caring and listening, you help others feel and release their pain. You develop your eloquence and descriptive powers to expand your language of feeling.

Opposite Pisces on the astrological mandala is the sign of Virgo. Pisces dissolves boundaries; Virgo draws boundary lines. In engaging Virgo exactitude to counter a spacey Pisces Moon, you learn to be more contained while holding space for others. You also discover how to facilitate conversations about feeling, to hone any psychic abilities you may have, and to develop an expression of the raw material of feeling through the structured medium of art—maybe something as structured as knitting or building with wood or maybe working through the earthy rigor of a specific dance technique.

EVOLVING Your extraordinary emotional sensitivity allows others to express themselves with full feeling and trust. You can be a container for intense sharing, which can lead to great breakthroughs and revelation. Your connection to the collective unconscious and the psychic realms assists people in creating magical possibilities.

Practices for the Moon • • • • • • • • •

Dive In

Draw two circles on a page. In one circle, name all the emotions you're very comfortable expressing. In the other circle, put the emotions that—for whatever reason—you have trouble sharing with others.

Now, write out what would help you start expressing/sharing *all* of these emotions. What gets in the way of expressing? What do you need support with to share them? What is the best thing that could possibly happen for you through investigating the range of emotions that lives inside of you? What are your historic sabotaging ideas about feelings/emotions that get in the way of their being fully expressed?

Reach Out

Get together with a close ally and share with them your emotional "training" and have them share theirs. Who taught you how to feel? What was acceptable? What was unacceptable? How do you adhere to those rules now? What are the four strongest emotional memories of your life? What makes them strong? What was functional or dysfunctional about those memories? What do you need to be absolutely confident to express all your feelings safely and maturely?

Or:

Host a screening of the film *Inside Out*, a highly entertaining Pixar flick that does an amazing job of depicting the complexity of every person's emotional life. Have each person talk about what feelings they relate to the most. Which feelings tend to sit at the "control panel"? How skillful do they feel at expressing all the different feelings?

Risk It

Find someone in your life from whom you have withheld your feelings out of fear. Let them know that you have a communication for them, but only if they are interested. Then, take full responsibility for your unspoken feelings. Say what you feel in a completely accountable way. For example: You tell the board president of your organization how much you admire their dedication and consistency in their role but also how you feel overwhelmed and uncomfortable in receiving frequent morning calls before 8:00 a.m. You explain that you were scared to say something because you didn't want to seem ungrateful or unappreciative of their efforts on behalf of the organization.

Reflect

Feel it. Go into nature without any distracting devices. Feel into and inhabit the experience of a tree, a boulder, a flower. Feel what it might feel being with you. Feel the *relationship*.

Talking Circle Questions

Gather with one or more people who have read this chapter. Using a talking piece everyone has agreed on (see note to "Talking Circle Questions" in chapter 2), have each person answer the following questions, one at a time. Make sure there is no cross-talk or side-talk; this is a time for completely undistracted, uninterrupted sharing. Before beginning, agree to keep what is said in the circle confidential, to listen deeply, to speak without rehearsing, and to be aware of time so that all have a chance to answer each question in the time available.

1. Tell about a time when you really shut down your feelings. Why did you?

2. Tell about a time when you had a huge emotional release that ended well.

3. Name the conditions in which you are really free to express full-throttle, deep emotions.

4. What do you do that helps you walk back from the ledge of difficult feelings? Name all your strategies.

5. Name at least one way you intend to call up the opposite energy in the astrological mandala to balance your Moon.

6. Share appreciations to each person in the circle for their ability to express themselves.

I will love the light for it shows me the way,
yet I will endure the darkness for
it shows me the stars.

OG MANDINO

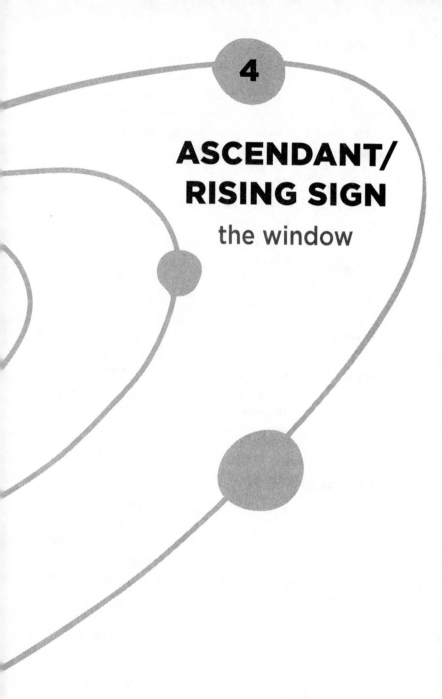

4

ASCENDANT/ RISING SIGN

the window

Your *ascendant* is the sign that was on the horizon the moment you were born, and it is one of the most important factors in the birth chart. Every sign of the zodiac is "ruled" by one of the planets, and the archetype of that planetary ruler is the "ruler" of your entire birth chart.

THE ASCENDANT AS MASK

The rising sign has traditionally been seen in astrology as a reflection of the "mask" you wear—of your most prominent persona now and of the role you played in your family system while growing up.

WINDOW

You can think of the ascendant more as a window: a window to your soul through which you see the essence of others. Fully inhabiting the skillful qualities of your rising sign makes you more accessible to others and able to more transparently see and experience others.

RISING SIGNS

How you occur to other people at first impression and the roles in which you tend to be cast in your family of origin and in your life in general are represented in the rising sign. It's interesting to note that certain physical characteristics are consistent with different signs on the ascendant; I share those characteristics in the listing for each sign.

Aries Rising

The person with Aries on the ascendant can come across as immature, fierce, and pushy—larger than life, physically commanding, with a potential for bullying behavior. Skillfully expressed, the radiant energy of this persona reads as powerful generosity. Folks with Aries rising tend to have large foreheads, ruddy faces, and youthful, athletic builds.

Aries rising means the chart is ruled by Mars, the planet of getting things done—and of anger and aggression.

PRIMITIVE　"Bulldozer" is your name, and bullying to get your way is your game. You look and act like a pugilist, and others find you insufferably aggressive. Pushing is second nature to you; being first is a necessity. No one had better ask you to consider them—you're focused on your path, and the job of others is to either do what you say or get out of your way.

ADAPTIVE　You possess a laudatory vitality of body and spirit. You appear strong, bold, and willing to help others in their quests. You listen deeply before acting and make sure your interactions are mutually beneficial. Others feel enlivened in your presence.

EVOLVING　Your aura is one of hugely bright light and solidity. Youthfulness and innocence pervade your interactions, even as you show up with maturity and experience. Your appearance and self-care encourage others to be fit and deeply self-loving. You create many opportunities in relationship for others to be central and highlighted.

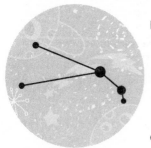

Bud, who has Aries rising, is a carpenter who has been building houses for thirty years. When he started out, he would lose his temper regularly and "spit nails." Every frustration felt intensely personal to him. Coworkers complained about his mood. At thirty-five, he hit his girlfriend while in a domestic dispute, which led Bud to an arrest and anger management courses. He learned so much there that he ended up volunteering to help lead groups.

Now, Bud is a great leader at work. Employees he supervises love working for him. He teaches his crew how to manage their emotions on the job, and they take this knowledge home to support their relationships with their partners and children.

Taurus Rising

Taurus rising people tend to occur as grounded, steady, and sensual. Less skillful ways to express this persona can come through in being mired down in the materialistic and in the stubborn impulses of this sign. Physically, they tend to have a serene gaze and to be muscular and dense or otherwise sturdily built. These people can have extraordinary physical charm and appeal.

Taurus rising means that elegant Venus rules the chart.

PRIMITIVE   Sluggish and thick, you move as though you're wading through oatmeal. You covet name-brand fashion, envying those who already have your next obsession in hand until you can get your hands on it yourself. Material consumption occupies much of your attention, but the last thing you want to do is work for those shiny objects you so desire.

ADAPTIVE   Your luscious body and style are joys for all to behold. You are completely at home in your being and exude a steady confidence. People come to you to rest in divine assuredness.

EVOLVING   You represent the attainment of heaven on earth. Your physicality recalls a temple of pristine art, and your social graces are stellar. As you move through life with impeccable timing and elegance, everyone with whom you interact feels warmly embraced and completely safe.

Gemini Rising

The person with Gemini rising comes across to others as intellectual, abstract, witty, and chatty. They tend to focus on their immediate social circles, wanting to learn about and interact with them as much as they can. Unskillful Gemini rising folks may have difficulty with focus, direction, and follow-through; the external expression of this internal challenge could yield a "mad professor" affect that may be sweet, charming, and interesting but not inspiring of trust from others. There is a kind of keen focus in the eyes and features of those with this placement.

Gemini rising means that chatty, mercurial Mercury rules the chart.

PRIMITIVE   You look and act disheveled and distracted—like a bunch of wires all ungrounded, flying in different directions. You are so careless with your speech that people avoid you; they know your monologue has no point and no end.

ADAPTIVE You look and act intelligent—sophisticated, even. You use your words carefully and distill your sharing to what is relevant to your audience. People love your breezy wit and cleverness, and they know you are capable of and ready for a more grounded, direct conversation when one is called for.

EVOLVING Like a master orchestral conductor, you are able to articulate exceptionally well and guide others in truly egalitarian conversation. You know just the right words and tone for the moment. People come to you to play an exquisite game of meaningful, impactful sharing.

Cancer Rising

Emotional, maternal, deeply caring and connected, empathic: that's the first impression made by most people with this placement. Its downsides can be moodiness and a need to be handled with extreme care to avoid emotional outbursts and tantrums. Cancer rising people have a yummy, welcoming look.

Cancer rising means the chart is ruled by the moody, emotionally present Moon.

PRIMITIVE Your specialties are being babied and involuntarily merging with others. Your emotional shell is so fragile that if others accidentally crack your nail or offend you, you'll cry a moon river. Your moody, broody ways take over the room like a toxic vapor.

ADAPTIVE Your heightened emotional maturity provides stable ground for others. You are physically and psychologically safe and alluring. Your cultivated sensitivities make you an expert listener and a loving, trustworthy confidant.

EVOLVING Everyone wants to be embraced by your halo of divine kindness and empathy. Your luminous appearance showers others with magic dust, elevating their own sense of cosmic belonging to a new level.

Leo Rising

Loving creativity, wholehearted expression, a bent toward performance—these all come standard with this rising sign. So, too, can a need to consume the entire spotlight and to be the center of attention, no matter what. The Leo rising person will often sport a "mane" of hair and have broad shoulders and a regal, graceful physicality.

Leo rising means the Sun rules the birth chart.

PRIMITIVE You will stop at nothing to get as much attention as possible—even if you have to look ridiculous, you'll get *everyone* to notice you. You expend lots of energy ensuring that all conversations circle back to the core of the matter: *you*. If another, for any reason, doesn't recognize you, they'll pay a price—and even then, you'll continue to ramp up, insistent on being acknowledged.

ADAPTIVE Your appearance and personality radiate creative, heartfelt sharing. Your light shines brightly not only for its own sake but also to shine upon others' self-expressions. With you, others feel a bountiful gaiety that amplifies life's every small joy.

EVOLVING You are the heartbeat of any group or gathering. Your essence sparkles so strongly that others feel called into their personal best as soon as they are in your presence. The sheer innocence of your love for life engenders a childlike wonder in everyone.

Virgo Rising

Under the best of circumstances, the Virgo rising native shows up resourced, capable, organized, and ready to help. Less skillful Virgo rising folks may lose sight of the proverbial forest while persevering on (and being critical of) the trees. Their appearance is very particular and pointed, with either high attention paid to hygiene and impeccable appearance or a resignation to slovenliness.

Like Gemini rising, Virgo rising means that Mercury rules the birth chart.

PRIMITIVE You look like a jumbled jigsaw puzzle. You are so caught up with cutting life into pieces that you have forgotten that there may be a simpler, gentler way. You hunt for your own and others' flaws. If you aim your hatchet at someone, they'll feel minced to smithereens.

ADAPTIVE You are an example of impeccable dress and comportment. Your looks are a coordinated symphony of sophistication. You seek every opportunity to serve with discernment and empathetic enfolding. Your refined style of service is both humble and proficient.

EVOLVING You are known for your mastery of compelling conversations and intelligent contributions, and you excel at bringing out the acuity and marvelousness of others. Your service is award-worthy, yet you constantly defer rewards to others. Your self-acceptance is so pure that others feel the wounds inflicted by their inner critics healed in your presence.

Libra Rising

The Libra rising native can show up as elegant and pulled together and can appear to others as exceedingly easy to get along with—a diplomatic and harmonious collaborator. Less skillful Libra rising folks can get stuck in concerns about looking good, pleasing others, and being liked. On the exterior, this placement usually means symmetrical facial beauty or a look that is otherwise remarkable and charming.

Like Taurus rising, the Libra rising chart is ruled by Venus.

PRIMITIVE You look and act like a doll on display. What others think about how you appear rules your life. Your baseline social tactic is to get others to like you, no matter what it costs your soul. You live for flattery and attraction.

ADAPTIVE Your harmonious, tasteful appearance and behavior inspire the standards of others. Your exceptional social graces support you in being taken seriously for your inner gifts. People feel truly seen by you.

EVOLVING You are a palette of aesthetic grandeur. Your style and social exchanges are photo-worthy in terms of both substance and the celestial awe evoked by your way of being.

Scorpio Rising

Sexy, mysterious, transformative, intense, deeply supportive, inspiring: that's Scorpio rising showing up in its strength. Suspicious, emotionally cautious, and reluctant to be close: that's Scorpio rising's less skillful expression. An intense gaze (one that doesn't reveal what is going on internally) usually comes with this placement: the power to look through others like an emotional X-ray machine.

Scorpio rising charts are ruled by transformative, depth-seeking Pluto.

PRIMITIVE You look and act like a venomous snake. Others should be very afraid—you can strike them down in an instant. Your eyes burn into and through their souls. And yet, you are deathly afraid of your own shadow; you self-soothe by projecting upon and judging others so they feel like there is something totally unlovable and unfixable about them.

ADAPTIVE Your steady and consistent offer of unconditional acceptance for your lesser-loved parts transforms those parts into newly found strengths. You see into others' immense, enduring talents and nurture them into manifestation.

EVOLVING Your drop-dead sexiness calls people to own their "wow" power, daring them to live from their wild, creative place. Securing others in a sense of invincible vulnerability is your specialty. People come to you to empower their mojo.

Sagittarius Rising

Sagittarius rising people tend to show up as confident and courageous, invested in truth, higher learning, and adventure. On rougher days or during rougher life periods, this fiery sign can confer impulsivity and overconfidence. This placement is especially known for blurting. Physically, it might show up as a strong and athletic build—horselike, with long legs.

Sagittarius rising charts are ruled by the expansive planet Jupiter.

PRIMITIVE Puffed up and bloviating, you fling words like arrows, and you boast about anything. Sloppy and impulsive, you run roughshod over people's feelings like an untamed horse, and you can't be bothered to pick up the mess you leave behind.

ADAPTIVE   You are a troubadour of integrity and wisdom. Your positive outlook and affirmation of others help heal the community. You look and act like a courageous adventurer in the land of learning and meaning.

EVOLVING   You are a fountain of sage counsel. Your very presence and energy help others believe in themselves, and people come from all over for your support in renewing their faith in their own abilities. Your generosity of spirit floods the community with light.

Capricorn Rising

The Capricorn rising native can appear either as a highly responsible, reliable, steadfast protector or as superior, defensive, and condescending. Capricorn rising people are the most concerned with having the right fashion at the right time. Physical steadiness and serious expressions are typical for this placement.

The charts for Capricorn rising natives are ruled by the stern and disciplined Saturn.

PRIMITIVE   Your facade is made of granite. If defensiveness were a badge, you would wear it. Your concern for your own social standing adheres to you like a glue stick. You assume that others feel inferior to you.

ADAPTIVE   You look and act like a protective parent. People rely on you to be well prepared and to embrace their concerns with kindness. You are exceptionally gifted at adding lasting value to any conversation.

EVOLVING You are a bastion of self-approval. You live the highest standards with vulnerability and patience. Communities depend on you to show them sustainable methods of self-care and interdependence.

Aquarius Rising

Unskillfully expressed, Aquarius rising can show up as unconventional—strange for strange's sake—and unfeeling, prone to hurtful blurts and an air of superiority. The Aquarius rising native can grow into their originality, genuineness, and all-encompassing love for the collective. These natives tend to appear very friendly, open, accessible, and accepting.

Aquarius rising charts are ruled by the surprising, innovative planet Uranus.

PRIMITIVE You look and act like an eccentric robot. Your lack of sensitivity to others is legendary. You are too far above the human fray to deal with actual people—and that's for the best, because you would rather be in sterile thought than to feel anything.

ADAPTIVE Your open face and smile are great welcomers. Your authentic and innovative take on things is refreshing. You bring fresh air to every interaction.

EVOLVING You are a globe of total unconditional love. People feel a sense of true belonging around you. You light up conversations with a genuine spark of creative genius.

As a teenager, Aquarius rising Saucy was known for cursing out her teachers and spending a lot of time incurring disciplinary actions. She dropped out of high school, saying it was too boring to be worthwhile. She spent some time backpacking around the country and became fascinated with organic farming. Her study and practice of biodynamic farming eventually led her to grow extremely high-quality marijuana. Today, she is a multimillionaire in Colorado, running a number of pot farms. She has also become a great philanthropist, donating money and sitting on boards of organizations helping the homeless in Denver.

Pisces Rising

People with this placement can—in unskillful moments—show up as lost or numbed out, with a tendency toward escape and victimhood. More skillful expression shines out empathy, sensitivity, and the softness and emotional safety of a calm tropical sea. A tranquil expression and flowing, dancer-like physicality are common with Pisces rising folks.

Pisces rising charts are ruled by the oceanic planet Neptune.

PRIMITIVE   You look and act like a drowning fish. Formless and feckless, you float and merge without noticing how lost you are. Sliding into altered states, you bypass true feelings for the numbness of escape. Losing yourself in another person is your cup of tea.

ADAPTIVE   Fluid and adaptable, you look and feel like a stunning dancer. You move with such refined trust that others want to bathe in your charisma. You are a shore of calmness for life's waves.

EVOLVING   You are like pure water; you bring pristine clarity to any interaction. Your innate smoothness and softness invite others to be unguarded and inspired, and your natural and enlightened compassion transform and heal the community.

Practices for the Rising Sign • • • • • •

Dive In

If there were a window to your soul that also looks into others' souls, how would you describe it in words? Make a sketch or find a picture somewhere that depicts your ideal window.

Reach Out

Ask six people you know to tell you three adjectives that describe how you come across when people first meet you.

Now, let each of those people know how you would *like* to come across. Get some feedback about how you can be more consistent in the impression you make on others.

Risk It

Spend an hour one day walking in a crowded part of town. Make real nonverbal contact with at least thirty people. Imagine it's the last day of your life and that these "strangers" truly matter to you.

See them. Let them see you.

Make notes on your field project and tell someone you know what you learned.

Reflect

Consider: How have you misjudged people in the past based on first impressions? What part of you was looking at them? What stopped you from seeing who they really were?

Also consider: Have you been misjudged in a quick appraisal? How did that feel? How would you like others to see you? How would you like to see others from now on?

Talking Circle Questions

Gather with one or more people who have read this chapter. Using a talking piece everyone has agreed on (see note to "Talking Circle Questions" in chapter 2), have each person answer the following questions, one at a time. Make sure there is no cross-talk or side-talk; this is a time for completely undistracted, uninterrupted sharing. Before beginning, agree to keep what is said in the circle confidential, to listen deeply, to speak without rehearsing, and to be aware of time so that all have a chance to answer each question in the time available.

1. Who do you see when you look in the mirror? How has that changed over the years?

2. What do you notice first about people, and why? What would you like people to notice first about you?

3. When do you feel most yourself with others?

4. If you were not scared at all, what parts of you would you express in social environments?

5. Tell each person in the group one thing that stands out about their presence.

6. If you had a magic wand and could create any lasting first impression of yourself, what would it be?

Words are wind.

GEORGE R. R. MARTIN

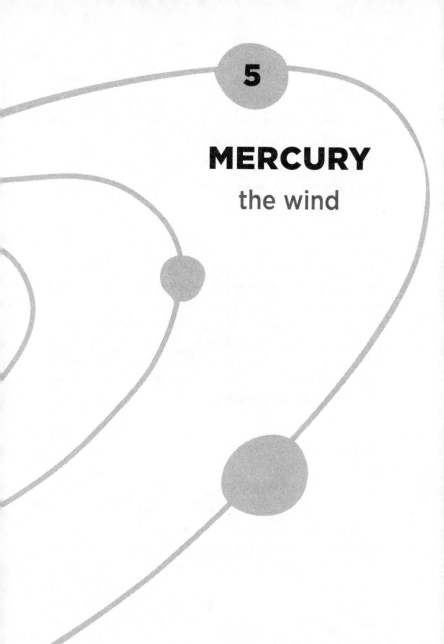

5

MERCURY
the wind

Mercury represents mind, thought, and the movement of ideas through any form of communication. It governs our abilities to learn, communicate, and conceptualize through language.

THE MYTH OF MERCURY

The ancient Roman god Mercury was the son of Jupiter. He was god of the winds and messenger for the gods. His mental quickness was so prodigious that he is said to have built his own lyre in the morning, right after being born, and to have mastered the instrument by noon that same day; by night, he'd managed to steal some cattle from the god Apollo.

Mercury oversaw commerce, spoken or written communication, and the business dealings of merchants and thieves. Mercury was also believed to be responsible for guiding souls to the underworld. Depictions of him in painting and sculpture usually include wings affixed to his feet or his hat.

THE WIND

Wind carries sound, materials, dreams, and fantasies all around the world. The flexibility, the alacrity, the clarity of air moving is mesmerizing. Using the image of the wind to represent Mercury moves the communication and networking aspect of Mercury from identification with a personified figure into a sense that all information and knowledge are truly free.

Just like the wind, everything we speak of and share through words is ephemeral and subject to interpretation. What is the purpose of the wind? To clear the air, remove toxins, carry seeds, allow for flight with updrafts. Wind can be exhilarating, but it can also be quite destructive, as in hurricanes, tornadoes, cyclones, and typhoons.

We've all felt the extraordinary harm of being in a tornado of hate language; we've also felt the exhilaration of being uplifted by words that elevate and inspire. Although we cannot control the wind, we can be conscious of directing our own use of moving air through words and connections.

MERCURY IN THE SIGNS

Mercury in the chart relates to communication, mind habits, and patterns. It denotes how we process information and communicate it, as well as the style in which we need to be communicated with in order for us to be enrolled.

Mercury in Aries

People with Mercury in Aries tend to communicate courageously, boldly, and directly, and they like to be at the receiving end of these same kinds of communication. Of themselves, they expect directness and clarity of thought, without a lot of meandering, stillness, or open space. They can become impatient with a lack of powerful, purposeful intention in themselves and in others.

PRIMITIVE You can become a battle-ax: in this expression, communication is a weapon, and might equals right. You speak before thinking, and aggressive thinking can dominate your relationships. You also tend to be incredibly impatient with other people speaking and equally impatient with your own mind. At the worst, you won't tolerate any obstacles against your goals or intentions; when those come up, you quit—but not before throwing a big tantrum.

ADAPTIVE   You speak on behalf of those who have a less powerful voice than yours—not by taking over for them but by directly inviting them into the conversation. You strongly seek balance in giving and taking around talking and sharing. You recognize that you have forceful opinions, and you modulate the tone of your voice so you can be heard without being perceived as a bully.

EVOLVING   Your heroic, courageous ways of communicating inspire everyone to take up their own causes. You can tap into the innate strength of each person's convictions and help them cultivate their words as actions in the world.

My friend Tate, whose Mercury is in Aries, was raised in a military family in which aggressive speaking was common and expected. He learned while young that to be heard, he had to be loud and brash. He also learned that by being the most verbally pushy person in the room, he could get his way.

As life went on, Tate's closest people—including his wife and his children—distanced themselves from him because they didn't want to be around his tone of rage. Tate started a long journey of introspection that led him to realize that his Mercury in Aries was best used to protect the people he loved from aggression and harm, not to inflict it upon them. He changed his habit from "Hear what I have to say!" to "Let me hear what you have to say."

Mercury in Taurus

The challenge of having Mercury in Taurus is using the steady, constant, productive energy of Taurus effectively in communication. Learning to use Mercury in Taurus skillfully requires that it be done through the earthy, concrete, sensual lens of this sign. Mastery here can bring extraordinary skill in singing and oration.

PRIMITIVE You can become turgid, stuck, and stubborn in the ways you think and communicate. Your communications can feel like cement walls, demarcating a place for others to stop pressing for more information or risk being pushed up against that wall, uncomfortably. You tend to speak slowly and ponderously, as if you were massaging every word, causing others to lapse into boredom and disconnection. You have trouble seeing communication as a dance. Yours more strongly resembles a statue; in fact, talking to you can feel a little like talking to a rock. And it isn't any easier inside your head: rather than flights of mental fancy, your thought processes can feel stuck in thick mud.

ADAPTIVE You plan what you're going to say, and you say it succinctly, with eye contact and acute awareness of the other person's interest level. You are faithful to what you believe and talk about it in a measured way, while also holding genuine curiosity about alternative viewpoints. You do not hold your opinions as fixed, unalterable objects but as conversations in flux and open to influence. You speak beautifully and with real attention to the quality and essence of your voice.

EVOLVING The sheer beauty and elegance of your communication invites others to see the positive possibility of language as an art form. Through you, language and communication become mirrors for other people's beauty, capacity, and intellectual competence.

Mercury in Gemini

In Gemini, Mercury is most at home; this placement offers great potential for abundant, easeful communication. The challenge is to maintain some kind of order and limits around it to avoid becoming an overintellectualizing "floating head." The aim is to use this native gift for ideas and thought for the benefit of all, rather than letting the winds of Mercury blow without any organizing principles that make its gifts receivable by others.

PRIMITIVE   You are like dust in the wind. You speak at length without substance, parameters, or containment. You hastily, sloppily throw words about as if they had no weight or import. This kind of blather and chatter is the source of the metaphors "hot air" and "airhead."

ADAPTIVE   You are able to cleverly, wittily, and humorously use words to break tension, invite conversation, and inspire inquiry. You develop a magical ability to connect the dots of ideas and grow to a place where you can skillfully help other people see where their values and ideas sit on common ground.

EVOLVING   You have become a master at seeing how people with disparate competencies and talents can come together for one cause. Like a laser beam, you home in on ways to express people's individual mental abilities; from there, you drop them into a spinning wheel of productivity that yields amazing outputs.

When Mercury in Gemini Natty was little, she often saw her parents fighting, and words were used as weapons. In her case, she decided to not speak up, and her incredible variety of ideas went underground. She experienced them in an internal tornado of frustration and repression. As she grew older, she was drawn to teaching and counseling, which provided her with safe, structured ways to communicate and bring people together. As she evolved, she became the executive director of a nonprofit organization in which her entire job was predicated on social and emotional communication that linked everyone to a common cause. Now, people often remark upon Natty's ability to speak into difficult and controversial topics with sensitivity and calm, thoughtful equanimity.

Mercury in Cancer

In this sign placement, communication and thought tend to focus on feelings. The journey from Primitive through Adaptive and Evolving expression is all about learning to name, manage, express, and channel emotions in healthy ways.

PRIMITIVE You might as well just put a pacifier in your mouth and make guttural whining noises. With Mercury in Cancer in its primitive state, your expressions tend to be variations on *baby, baby, baby me*—sometimes, even said with a baby voice. You often talk and think about your emotions, favoring a theme of the self-pity party: no one understands you, no one *gets* you, in part because they haven't realized your emotional genius. When people don't want to listen to your endless whimpering, you accuse them of being cruel.

ADAPTIVE   You have an admirable ability to feel other people's emotions, and you are adept at diving into conversations about all things emotional. You know how to address intellectual debate and commentary at the feeling level. You are able to go beneath people's defensiveness and to speak right to their vulnerability.

EVOLVING   You can engage your community in compassionate empathy through persuasive, heartfelt conversation and speech. In any tense situation, you can defuse the conflict by going right into the needs of the inner child of everyone involved. You have a particular sensibility for seeing the positive implications of any feeling state, and you know how to reframe an unskillful feeling into a constructive request.

Mercury in Leo

Loving, expressive, creative communication is the hallmark of Mercury in Leo. It can also be either overly focused on "me, me, me!" or, by turns, boastful and overly hungry for recognition. Channeling the fiery energy of Leo into spirited sharing of one's gifts with the world is the key to the Evolving expression of this placement.

PRIMITIVE   You can't stop talking about yourself. Somehow, every single topic is a reminder that it's all about you. Your obsessive need for words of adoration and admiration creates intense frustration for you and for others who can't meet the demand. Once you start telling a story about your life, all the air is sucked out of the room.

ADAPTIVE   You speak to the heart of the matter with grace and aplomb. You invite other people to share what's most valuable to them in terms of their love of life and of other people. You take every opportunity to acknowledge, appreciate, and brag about people in your life. Your words of joy are a fountain of inspiration for others.

EVOLVING   You are like a songbird of hope and promise for the future. When you put people together—whether in the same cozy room or in a huge convention hall—they are instantly linked at the heart. Your laughter is contagious and makes everyone glad to be alive.

Bobby, who has Mercury in Leo, grew up in a family of actors and artists. At a young age, he learned to compete with his relatives' intense narcissism through braggadocio and storytelling. By the time he was in college, he realized that his drunken monopolizing of the room might be earning him a lot of superficial attention but wasn't getting him the true love or career success he wanted. He decided to study the art of negotiation—both to be a better businessperson and to learn how to effectively bring out the heart of other people's concerns. He eventually became a corporate trainer who specializes in teaching others how to listen into the core of the matter with heart, compassion, and empathy. His friends know him as generous, open, and encouraging.

Mercury in Virgo

Virgo specializes in transforming chaos into order, and this placement for Mercury can mean either a hell of perfectionism and criticism toward self and others or a heaven of clear, concise, easy-to-relate, service-oriented ideas, practices, theories, or organizing principles.

PRIMITIVE You love to judge and criticize others' every move, but the joy you feel in holding others up to impossible, fussy, petty standards is short lived. Even as others suffer under your judgmental, nitpicky eye, you talk to yourself more contemptuously than anyone else can imagine. Your mind is clenched in a tight fist of complaint.

ADAPTIVE You use your developed analytical skills to help others realize their dreams. You see the imperfections in others' communications as an opportunity to embrace possibilities for further understanding. You think carefully before you speak so that your words add value to the conversation.

EVOLVING Your mind is a vehicle for service. You stay focused on how your gifts and talents can aid others and bring people together. You speak about people's essence and effort with brilliant brevity. You help untangle oppositional positions into conversations about shared ideals.

Mercury in Libra

This placement shepherds balanced communication that is focused on helping others see both sides of any issue. An emphasis on fairness and on synthesizing input from different corners makes the Mercury in Libra person an excellent negotiator who helps everyone feel heard and valued in any conversation, no matter how diverse the opinions that enter the picture.

PRIMITIVE   If anyone wants to postpone making a decision about anything, they know you're the person to talk to. You can go around and around all day, recognizing every possible angle on an issue without ever coming to a conclusion. The most terrifying notion would be to take even a hesitant step in the wrong direction. You're especially good at pulling others into a realm of airy cogitation right along with you.

ADAPTIVE   You begin to recognize that while a tapestry of thoughts and ideas is a thing of beauty, at some point, you have to take the risk of moving forward. You continue to help others feel heard in their positions, but you also marshal the will to crystallize a decisive plan that helps everyone feel included and valued.

EVOLVING   You become a calm, balanced voice in support of harmonious, beautiful collaboration. Others come to recognize that you can be counted on to hold the dualities that are inevitable in any conscious process of decision-making. They know they can call upon you to distill the genius of diverse positions into a coherent and balanced whole.

Mercury in Scorpio

Scorpio's lens facilitates communication and thought patterns that truly cut to the chase. There is potential here for incredible depth, incisiveness, and vulnerability. Along with the capacity to see to the deepest heart of things and bring the story of that depth to others, this placement brings a need to act with empathy and care. It can be used to do incredible harm or to bring transformative help.

PRIMITIVE   Cruelty and meanness have found their spokesperson. You allow yourself to rage and spew at others, and you take no responsibility for the harm this does. You harbor resentments and secrets, holding them close like unexploded bombs until it's time for everyone else to feel their heat. You withhold as a way of punishing others.

ADAPTIVE   You have a laser-like problem-solving mind. Others know they can come to you for ethical help. Your words are both transformative and empathetic. Your conversations with others assist in deepening their truth and vulnerability.

EVOLVING   Your courageous speech engages people's truest convictions and supports them to tap into fearless commitment. You are able to be transparent and vulnerable without compromising your personal power and potency.

Garland has Mercury in Scorpio. As a child, they were obsessed with horror and monstrous stories; at that time, the intrusion of murderous, dark, envious thoughts into their psyche caused them to feel ashamed, as though they had a dark secret to keep from the rest of the world. When Garland went to college, they found they had an incredible love for forensic psychology. That's when their obsession with crime shows and horror films began to make sense.

They trained in forensic medicine and became one of the world's foremost experts in criminal forensic psychology.

This application of Mercury in Scorpio—a constructive way to use their talent for looking into the darkest recesses of the human experience—allowed them to be more balanced, easygoing, and joyful in ordinary life.

Mercury in Sagittarius

Mercury in Sagittarius suggests fiery, direct, outspoken communication and thought. It can mean being quick to judge and to state your position with authority—even when it may not be founded in anything besides your personal agenda. You often think that you know best what is best for everyone else.

PRIMITIVE You are righteous, imperious, and superior. The subtext of much of your communication is, "I have the right beliefs, you idiot! Let me tell you, in a long-winded way, how to live your life better." You just shoot from your mouth and don't much care how the bullets land.

ADAPTIVE You can speak truth to power with humility and openness. People rely on you for generous, authentic appraisals of things. You honor your word and practice mindful speech. When you lapse into the primitive habit of striking out, you catch yourself, take responsibility, and try again to communicate thoughtfully and with equanimity.

EVOLVING Your words evoke liberatory impulses in the collective. The stories you tell hit the sweet spot of relevance and meaning. All are inspired by your ability to speak to the deepest truths joyfully and to raise the full cup of gratitude.

Mercury in Capricorn

With Mercury in Capricorn, communication and thought tend toward habits of practicality, advance planning, consideration of consequences, foresight, and dividing things into categories.

PRIMITIVE   You speak coldly, tersely, and condescendingly to others. They clearly don't get it. You can't be bothered to listen to them because you already know what they're going to say. You're locked in your mental positions. You don't have time to address anyone's feelings. You just want to *get stuff done!*

ADAPTIVE   You use your highly practical perspective to contribute to the conversation. You walk your talk impeccably. You think clearly and methodically and offer reasonable solutions when asked. Your ability to name and tame emotions is great; therefore, you are able to de-escalate conflict when it occurs. You can be counted on as a calm mind in the midst of any interpersonal storm.

EVOLVING   Your thoughts go toward long-term planning and required steps for the realization of complex visions. You are able to hear others' concerns and organize them in such a way that they feel they've been heard and acknowledged. Your care inspires others to new ideas about how to proceed. You take full responsibility for your mistakes and do all you can to make things right again, and you teach others (both explicitly and by example) the incredible power of these restorative practices.

Stella, whose Mercury is in Capricorn, grew up in a facts-only type of family. At the dinner table, Stella was quizzed on her vocabulary and was put down for any type of unsubstantiated comment. She was taught to be practical and to approach mental and emotional challenges with a utilitarian frame of mind.

Although in the rest of Stella's chart she had extraordinary artistic gifts, she ended up making her living writing nonfiction. Stella learned that she could employ her logical, methodological thinking process to write cogent, clear, accessible articles and books. She also realized that in personal relationships, a hard-facts approach was not appealing; so, she studied how to be socially and emotionally connected. As she became a respected expert in the field of social-emotional learning, she practiced what she preached. In her family, social circles, and community, she became well known as someone who could speak, listen, empathize, and connect, and she became a trusted resource and friend to many.

Mercury in Aquarius

Here, communication and thought tend toward a bird's-eye overview—a visionary capacity to see what really matters for the collective and to plan around the big picture. This elevated perspective comes with liabilities, especially in terms of more intimate communication: there can be a dismissing of interpersonal differences and a disrespecting of individual intelligences that are not your own.

PRIMITIVE You know everything there is to know; you don't need to learn a thing. Your views are obviously right, so no one should even bother to correct you. If you say it, it *must* be true because you have a direct connection to the only source that matters: yourself. If anyone thinks you're stubborn, it's only because they are idiots.

ADAPTIVE   You have an eagle's-eye impartiality that allows you to see things in big-picture mode. This enables you to synthesize a useful overview of any situation and to do so from many perspectives. Your conversations tend to include everyone who wants to participate because you embrace and celebrate diversity of opinion. When you recognize that you are mistaken, you eagerly admit it; your core motivation is to learn as much as you can to be of service to the collective.

EVOLVING   You recognize the fact that the group mind is only as good and clear as it is facilitated for the highest good of all. You accept that the gift of your communication skills equips you well to do this kind of facilitation, and you seek out every opportunity to weave the stories of individuals into a vital, connected, cohesive map. You use your immense intuition to bring people together for causes and movements that will transform the world. Your greatest joy comes through helping others realize their dreams of unity and community.

Mercury in Pisces

It can be a challenge to ground into logical communication and linear thought through the Pisces perspective. The sign of Pisces is all about boundlessness—afloat in a watery, imagistic world. It can be so hard to communicate from this placement that it can feel tempting to escape into your own withdrawn realm. Developing skillful expression of and through this placement requires channeling your loving, vivid sensitivity with care and generosity.

PRIMITIVE   Your mind is one big fog bank. You cannot focus on anything! You spend hours chasing your own tail, and then you remember you don't even *have* a tail. Escape is your best friend; you can easily drown in distractions. When feelings override your ability to speak (which happens often), you just check out and disassociate. Your mental life is all about fantasy, and you use this as an excuse to not keep your word.

ADAPTIVE   Your exquisite sensitivity aids others in being more genuine and authentic. Your rapturous speaking voice invites people into your particular aesthetic of communication. When you speak truth to power, others can *feel* your words. Your ability to tell a great story is like a dream come true.

EVOLVING   You channel divine love for all of creation. Your connection with higher dimensions allows you to see others' potential and speak directly to their inspired qualities. People come to you from all over to feel safe, seen, and celebrated. You are a model of social and emotional intelligence; you ground others who want to escape by inviting them into your experience of heaven on earth.

Practices for Mercury • • • • • • • • • •

Dive In

Keep a thought diary for a day: Every hour, write down the most prevalent theme of your thoughts. Note whether you are focused on what you want to be thinking about.

Or:

Keep a speaking-out diary for a day. Every hour, note what you speak about the most and what you do not speak about at all. Do you like what you observe?

Reach Out

Write a letter to someone you have been underappreciating. Let them know about all the positive thoughts you are having about them. This will actually boost your mood and positively adjust the emphasis of your thoughts.

Gather with friends or loved ones to watch the movie *The Matrix* or the series *Sense8*—both of which are about the power of thoughts and feelings and the interconnected nature of all thoughts and feelings happening in all minds and hearts. Discuss how much you can attune to one another's thoughts and feelings. Talk about the extent to which each of you feels like your thoughts are not your own.

Ask a few important people in your life to reflect on these questions: What topics do they hear you speak of most? Do they imagine there are some topics about which you could speak out more often?

Risk It

Take one deeply held perspective in your life. Spend three days striving to see it from the opposite point of view. Experience this as an intentional practice and return to it often. This practice will help you get into the head and thoughts of someone who thinks very differently from you. When the three days have passed, write a page on what you learned and how it can improve your point of view.

Reflect

Spend a few hours studying the lyrics of songs you love. Determine what they all have in common. Let this show you how you may be subconsciously feeding patterns of thought that do not serve you or that you care about.

Talking Circle Questions

Gather with one or more people who have read this chapter. Using a talking piece everyone has agreed on (see note to "Talking Circle Questions" in chapter 2), have each person answer the following questions, one at a time. Make sure there is no cross-talk or side-talk; this is a time for completely undistracted, uninterrupted sharing. Before beginning, agree to keep what is said in the circle confidential, to listen deeply, to speak without rehearsing, and to be aware of time so that all have a chance to answer each question in the time available.

1. What thoughts make you the happiest? What time in your life did you have those thoughts the most?

2. What thoughts disturb you? What conditions stir up those thoughts?

3. What words bring you into a peaceful state? How often do you use them?

4. What words cut you to the core when spoken aloud? Why?

5. Tell each person in the group at least two positive thoughts you have about them.

6. What is the easiest way to clear your mind and reset yourself toward gratitude?

Beauty is the only thing that time cannot harm.
Philosophies fall away like sand, creeds follow
one another, but what is beautiful is a joy for
all seasons, a possession for all eternity.

OSCAR WILDE

Let the beauty of what you love
be what you do.

RUMI

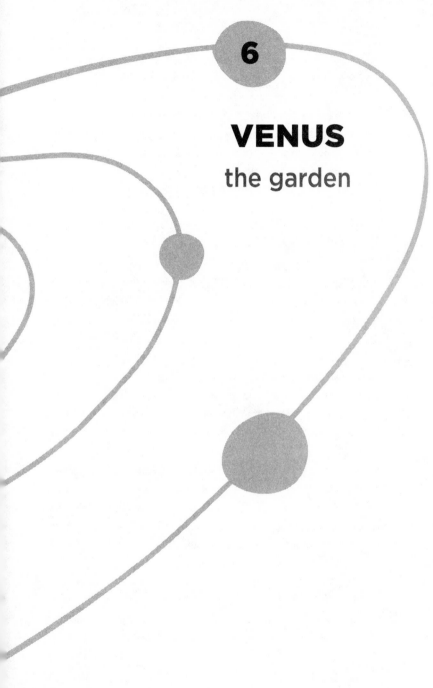

6

VENUS
the garden

Venus represents love and beauty. Its placement influences desire for social and romantic relationships, attraction to others, and having others attracted to you. Venus is in play wherever you feel drawn to artistic pastimes and other pleasures that are sensual and aesthetically pleasing. It represents the feminine principle—the expression of the feminine in each person's birth chart. The seeking of harmony in any area of your world or life is also ruled by Venus.

THE MYTH OF VENUS

Venus was the ancient Roman goddess of fertility, sex, love, and beauty. Her purview also included victory of all kinds, as well as prostitution. She is the Roman version of the Greek Aphrodite. Among her lovers were Vulcan (her husband) and Mars; her children by Mars were Timor, the fearful one; Metus, the terrifying one; Concordia, the harmonious one; and the Cupids, famously used to depict aspects of love in classical painting and sculpture. It's also said that she mothered Priapus, a minor deity most famous for his extremely large phallus. She also fell in love with mortals, including Adonis, for whose affection she competed with the goddess Persephone. (Zeus eventually had to step in to help the two goddesses negotiate an Adonis-sharing plan, which Adonis ignored in order to spend most of his time with Venus, until he met his end in a boar attack.) An affair with another mortal, Anchises, led to the birth of a son, Aeneas, who is said to be an ancestor of the founders of Rome, including Romulus, Remus, and Julius Caesar.

THE GARDEN

An idyllic garden has varied display of color and form and honors the natural cycles of seed, sprout, growth, bloom, and decay.

When expertly planted and with plants wisely placed in the most beautiful and symbiotic way, a garden allows for interdependency between species of plant and flower. The plants in such a garden can support one another, as well as the other creatures in the environment including pollinators, seed spreaders, and composters alike.

The beauty of the garden is not only in its solo standouts but also in the entirety of the tableau. It flourishes only through pristine care and thoughtfulness about the needs for nurturing, pruning, and cultivating. Tended to in this way, your Venus chart placement will illuminate your own radiance while complementing everyone in your context and proximity.

VENUS IN THE SIGNS

The sign in which Venus sits in your chart influences your desires, your appreciation of beauty, and your desire to create and cultivate beauty. Your Venus placement also reflects what you value—and therefore what you are attracted to.

Venus in Aries

People with this placement have the extraordinary capacity for self-possessed desires and needs—or a tendency toward self-obsessed considerations. The fiery, forward-moving drama of Aries brings courage and a will to act decisively in relationship. The strength of this placement can predispose one to "bull in a china shop"-style action and reaction; cultivating its skillful side requires building the capacity to hold and direct its energy productively.

PRIMITIVE You want what you want when you want it. If it serves you, great! If not, then you're not interested. You think about your own image obsessively and need others to admire and appreciate your independence. If others don't do what you want, you'll figure out a way to get it done yourself.

ADAPTIVE   You are the definition of feminine courage. Your goal in relationship is to bring out the autonomy in both you and another—an autonomy that makes both you and the other better. You are willing to stand for the less fortunate because you have the strength and conviction to see the current situation through to resolution. You can convince others to value themselves, even when they doubt their own worth.

EVOLVING   You are the person to stand in front of the firing line in order to create social harmony and justice. Nothing can stop you from ensuring that others' rights are protected and valued. In relationship, you take a clear stand for self-valuation and compassion. You are an exemplar of composed power and thoughtfulness.

Venus in Taurus

The deep sensuality of Taurus doesn't mind taking things slowly. There is great potential here for moment-to-moment presence and enjoyment of beauty, especially beauty found in or sourced from the natural world. If one's basic material needs aren't being met, however, this placement can predispose one to becoming preoccupied with getting more, more, more.

PRIMITIVE   Your clarion call: "Just give me more presents, damn it!" You don't have enough jewelry. You don't have enough toys. And you can't really be into another unless they have a lot of money. You will trade your self-respect for security in relationship.

ADAPTIVE   You know just how to create a sense of beauty and harmony in your connections. Your sensual, appreciative nature infuses the environment with an underlying garden of delights. Your loyalty and perseverance are unbounded when it comes to the people you love.

EVOLVING   You stand for the ecology of this planet and the healthy ecology of reciprocal relationships. You see everything as connected to bringing heaven to earth. Your desire for beauty surpasses the personal and becomes a means for everyone to be related to their own beautiful natures.

Althea, who has Venus in Taurus, grew up in a poor urban neighborhood but went to school with a group of highly privileged girls. She coveted their designer clothes, brands, and bags. She never felt she had enough of her own beauty capital. Althea realized, through the help of a mentor, that she had a deep desire to create beauty in her own life and on her own terms. She got her GED and started studying design and fashion. Althea's fullest expression of her Venus in Taurus came through her development of a unique fashion line that donates half its profits to young women who need clothing for proms and other important events.

Venus in Gemini

The sign of Gemini brings to the planet Venus a tendency toward abstraction and forward movement—a combination that can mean either airy flexibility and accommodation or distractibility and scatteredness.

PRIMITIVE "Do I like you? Don't I? I just can't make up my mind." That's the Gemini flavor of Venus. The grass is really greener over there—you just *know* it. You once were gay, but now you're bi, but actually you're really straight. You might have big plans you're thrilled about, but as soon as you receive a better offer? "Sorry—can't make it."

ADAPTIVE Meaningful conversation is your raison d'être. You bring a variety of people together to explore the value of interconnectedness. Your knowledge base of relating styles is vast, and you can easily tune into the core relational needs of others.

EVOLVING You can speak and write at elevated levels about the importance of interdependency and intimacy. You are a relied-upon consultant for groups working to create a dialogue that is rich and nourishing to all.

Venus in Cancer

With this placement, relationships are either a source of deep emotional nourishment or triggers for moodiness and sensitivity. The feeling self of those with Venus in Cancer is at the forefront when they make choices around relationship and around creating beauty and harmony in their surroundings. Emotions may be close to the surface; those with Venus in Cancer may feel their needs leading the way if they do not maintain an awareness of the common good and their role in creating it.

PRIMITIVE   You want others to be your mommy. *Really, you just need a mommy.* Why does anyone else have needs? If you don't get your way in this relationship, there will be a lot of whimpering, whining tantrums. Eating your feelings is one way you suppress your awareness of any responsibility you might have in your relationships.

ADAPTIVE   You channel divine Mother energy for others and for yourself. Your ability to see others' vulnerabilities and core needs is highly developed. With you, others find a safe haven in which they can depend on your trustworthiness and emotional solidity.

EVOLVING   People come to you from all over the world to receive a pure type of nurturing love that brings out their best. You inspire others' capacity to be nurturers themselves. In the lap of your exquisite care, people and groups feel contained, related, and inspired. Your home or environment is a sanctuary to which people can retreat to restore their soft animal bodies.

Leah, who has Venus in Cancer, lost her mother at an early age. She grasped desperately at other women as friends and mother figures to act as sources of security for her. As she did her deep personal work around the loss of her mother, she became one of the foremost healers in helping people work through their mother issues. In her personal life, Leah's friends have come to rely on her to create warm, comforting, nourishing home environments.

Venus in Leo

This placement suggests vitality, loyalty, warmth, playfulness, and generosity. Those with Venus in Leo are both flirtatious and unabashed about showing the world (especially any beloveds) how amazing they are. Courtship and romance are great focuses for their creativity and verve. When unskillfully lived out, people with this placement can bring unreasonably high expectations for how others should court and attend to them; rather than making others feel like the center of their attention, they need to be special dominants.

PRIMITIVE You insist that others just watch you dazzle them! It's not going to work out if they take their eyes off you for even a second because you're the star of this relationship. When others are with you, your very presence is enough: it's *A Star Is Born* every day. You find the drama of relationship to be way more entertaining than getting along. You may as well have invented the term *prima donna/primo uomo*.

ADAPTIVE Your heartfelt abilities to sense another's needs and desires helps you feel inspired and bonded. You are able to attach yourself to another's highest creative and amorous abilities and bring out romance in everyday life. You can weave a story of love from just about anything, and you take care to include the other as the star of that story.

EVOLVING You are the heartbeat of the friendships, relationships, and organizations of which you are a part. People feel incredibly loved and accepted in your presence. They feel their hearts expand and become more inclusive of all other people.

Venus in Virgo

The self-criticism that can come with Virgo placements can be projected into relationship, making it hard to let go in love and to let others fully into one's heart. Rather than letting go into expressions of romance, the "love language" of the Venus in Virgo person can center more on refining small details—doing it *right* rather than enjoying the ride for what it is.

PRIMITIVE   You are duty bound to let those in relationships know all about what they are doing wrong. You are a master at finding another's Achilles' heel and then kicking them in it. Sometimes your position is that no relationship is good enough for you, and so no one need apply. Once you have fully seduced an intimate partner, you get busy showing them, in all ways, how they are insufficient. You are ruthlessly self-critical about your own appearance, and you regularly tear yourself apart for perceived flaws, both large and small.

ADAPTIVE   You begin to show up as a self-possessed teacher of elevated relationship. You come to understand that your powers to serve are greater than any imperfection you see in yourself or in others. Your faith in others' ability to handle their own issues grows beyond any mind-imposed limitation.

EVOLVING   There is no task too little for you to do with humility in order to serve the greater good of interrelatedness. You come to see how every seeming mistake is a doorway to great opportunity for understanding between all people. People come to you for counsel—to be reminded of the bigger-picture beauty of the life cycle and the ways in which we all connect within it.

Katherine, with Venus in Virgo, grew up with a mother who was impossible to please. The standards for Katherine's beauty, composure, and comportment were unrealizable. This led Katherine to pick a partner in her first marriage who was critical and unforgiving. Through divorcing this partner, Katherine finally realized there was no point in being perfect. Not only was perfection unattainable; it also had no value in any real loving relationship. During a period when she purposely remained single, Katherine built her sense of self-love and self-worth enough that she could attract and choose someone who loved every single foible and flaw she had and who recognized the importance of this loving acceptance in her own happiness.

Venus in Libra

Kindness, fairness, and a willingness to compromise are all hallmarks of Venus in Libra. Venus is Libra's planetary ruler, so this is an easeful placement. It can pave the way for peaceful, harmonious, lifelong partnership. The downside can be Venus in Libra's tendency to try to make or keep the peace and harmony of a relationship, even if it means not delving into important individual issues—a prioritizing of the pair bond and of the other over one's own needs.

PRIMITIVE "What do you think of me? No, really! What do you think of me? How am I doing? Do I look good? Wait . . . I could look a *lot* better." You are never reassured that you are doing, saying, and being enough to be the perfect partner. You'll say or do almost anything in order to be liked. You overfocus on your looks, buying every cosmetic product you can get your hands on in order to be the most idealized paragon of elegant beauty.

ADAPTIVE   Your extraordinarily balanced perspective allows you and your significant other(s) to have a profound give-and-take on any relational issue. Your mediating skills are consistent with your values of peace and harmony in relationship. You accept your divine gift of beauty as a treasure to be taken care of through healthy, natural means.

EVOLVING   You surround people with beauty, harmony, and calm. People rely on you to bring in elegant wit and humor to defuse conflict. Your breath-of-fresh-air contributions allow everyone to pause and reflect on their own better natures.

Venus in Scorpio

With this placement, what matters most in relationship is depth, intensity, and passion. The Venus in Scorpio is willing to say or do whatever it takes to get profoundly connected, and they are more than willing to go into the darkest depths to stay in that realm with their beloveds.

The honor of having Venus in Scorpio native is in cultivating a sense of permanency with the impermanent. People with this placement can be the most loyal, devoted, and unwavering friends and lovers.

PRIMITIVE   For you, "'til death do us part" means "I'll kill you if I have to." You find a strange beauty in a mutual descent into depravity, and you find yourself mirrored in sad stories about destructive passions like *Leaving Las Vegas* and *Sid and Nancy*.

Your ability to hold a grudge and suffer silently with vengeance is surpassed by no one. With you, possession is elevated to an art form. You are *not* to be crossed.

ADAPTIVE   Nothing can stop you from loving your beloved with complete, transformative compassion. Your egoless commitment to love invites others to realize that there is nothing more precious on this Earth than our affinity for one another. You show others how to take the most difficult emotions and compost them into the flowering of self-love and understanding.

EVOLVING   You overcome insurmountable odds to evidence your love for the people you care about. No rainstorm, shitstorm, or other obstacle can keep you from your undying devotion to a higher love. Many people benefit from your invincible caring for community and inclusivity.

Venus in Sagittarius

This placement can set a person up for adventurous, larger-than-life, joyful relationships. The Venus in Sagittarius person tends toward growth and expansion through relationship and loves to party with others who have the same aims. It can mean needing more space in relationship or difficulty committing to one person completely. This placement confers craving for a sense of meaning and a constant pursuit of knowledge.

PRIMITIVE   You'd much rather party until you drop than have a deep conversation, and you have zero patience for anyone who tries to stop your party train. You ringlead risky adventures, mocking anyone who doesn't have the *cojones* to play along. Anyone who wants to be your lover is told right up front that you can't be expected to be faithful or loyal; if they want your love, they'll have to play the game of life your way. You don't care much about the carnage your party lifestyle leaves behind, as you are too caught up in the beauty of freedom.

ADAPTIVE   You recognize the importance of commitment and mutuality in love relationships. You know you're going to have to slow down and be present with beloveds if you're going to reap the rewards of lasting love. You begin to implement specific relationship strategies—maybe learned from a therapist, coach, or workshop or from one of the many excellent books on the topic.

EVOLVING   You come to recognize that beauty comes in packages both grand and small and that total freedom's flip side is the aching longing for deep intimacy. As you cultivate the ability to focus your considerable energies on a smaller scale, you discover that intimate relationships can hold your passion if you handle them with the deepest care. You still have fun and adventure—getaways, seminars, parties, and celebrations—but rather than driving the proverbial party bus off the cliff, you employ your strength and charisma in helping everyone feel safe *and* celebrated.

Marco has Venus in Sagittarius. He grew up on a farm, running free like a horse throughout his childhood. He traveled quite a bit with his family, and by the time he was eighteen, he'd had three lovers in three foreign countries. Marco's biggest issue is his conflict between wanting deep, meaningful love relationships and wanting ultimate freedom to not be tied down. It took Marco fifty years to realize that real freedom was the ability to commit to one person and to experience the depth of wisdom, sensuality, and intimacy when freedom comes through self-expression rather than through a variety of partners.

Venus in Capricorn

Skill with this placement can mean committed determination to serve and support others in relationship—in particular, the Venus in Capricorn person can be counted on to be an earthy, steady force in any emotional storm, helping guide the ship of intimate relationship to a safe harbor. The challenge here is to be protective instead of utilitarian and to be a steward instead of a manipulator.

PRIMITIVE   You prove your worth by being seen, heard, and talked about in relation to important people. Wherever you encounter someone who is famous, you pursue their affections shamelessly in order to justify your existence. You'll trade your self-respect for a high-status place, and this is the closest feeling you have to real intimate love. You don't love others; you love what they can do for you. Designer items like Hermès belts and Prada bags are your price tag for affection.

ADAPTIVE   Your steadfast and highly ethical commitments to love are notable, and your earnest admiration for others encourages them to do their best. As your self-respect deepens, you become more able to unclench yourself from your focus on appearances in order to value your relationships. Your standards for emotional reciprocity are high, and you'll climb over any mountain to preserve your intimate relationships—especially when you have taken vows.

EVOLVING   Your values in relationship are as secure and as grounded as a mountain. Your friends and family see you as a loving steward of the most loving vision of connection. Your humility and grace around what you have achieved allow others to shine, and you use your considerable influence and resources to uplift others. People often comment on how reliable and solid your love is, through fair or foul weather.

Venus in Aquarius

Through the lens of Aquarius, Venus wants to express itself through relationship at the level of community, to spread its loving big-picture vision to benefit as many people as possible. Beyond the one-on-one dyad or the single-family home, Venus in Aquarius knows there is a whole universe of potential for interrelatedness that follows its own set of rules.

PRIMITIVE   You just can't decide which hundred people you like best. Your need for unconventionality keeps you from being vulnerable and committed. Rules? What rules? You just "do" love any way you want, regardless of anyone else's feelings. When you are pushed for more intimacy, you just find some-one else to cherish you. If it's kinky, count you in.

ADAPTIVE   Friendship reaches new heights with this placement. *Agape* is your way of love; it allows others to feel completely accepted and treasured for all their facets. Your embrace reassures others that they are the stars of their own expanded universes. Loyalty is a cornerstone of your relational values. You readily host honoring conversations about full, positive self-expression.

EVOLVING   Your uncanny ability to intuit the needs of others provides you with the ability to knit individuals into a loving community. Your affinity with all types of people confirms your quest to bring love to a higher ground. Your community knows you as a loving guide who stands for democracy and equality. Your affection is easily and sincerely given; as it emanates from you, it fills the room with light.

Lydia, whose Venus is in Aquarius, grew up in a conservative household. Her parents wanted her to be married by the time she was twenty and to have three babies in tow by the time she was thirty. This was not Lydia's truth. By the time she went to school in Northern California, she found she had a radical taste for nonmonogamous relationships. She became part of an intentional polyamorous community and found her true happiness working actively in a space of equitable, nonpossessive, open relationships. She went on to become a pioneering podcaster whose offerings outlined the ethics, logistics, and potential ecstasies of living a polyamorous lifestyle.

Venus in Pisces

Watery, dreamy Pisces loves love and boundless intimacy; this placement makes possible fantastic flights of romantic fancy with no beginning and no end—flights that may feel more inviting in the imaginal realm than possible in the real world of actual people. It brings intense emotional vulnerability and a connection not only to immediate beloveds but also to all creation. Being a human sounding board for universal love and passion can be confusing and exhausting, possibly leading to a place of playing the victim or falling into addiction.

PRIMITIVE   Your fantasies of romance keep you from doing much else, including having a real connection. You don't want to be with another unless they rescue you from yourself. You would rather drown in addictions than face the real work of intimacy. "Don't bother me," you might be heard to say, "I am sleeping through this lifetime. No one could possibly be the Prince or Princess Charming I need."

ADAPTIVE   Your capacity for empathy is noteworthy. Your ideals of love include Achilles' heels and warts—your own and those of others. Your warmth heals others' hearts and creates the possibility for powerful tenderness. Others can count on you to go the distance because you know what unconditional love can do.

EVOLVING   Through your eyes, others are able to see that the world can live as one. Your peaceful heart exudes calmness and containment. Within you, others find the refuge of true spiritual sanctuary, where the mind stills and the heart expands. People gather around you to let go of defenses and to melt into the power of mercy.

Practices for Venus • • • • • • • • • •

Dive In

Make a chart of your love life, mapping its highs and lows from beginning to the present time. Next to the highs, describe what combination of factors created that state of bliss; next to the lows, name the painful conditions that contributed.

Now, rewrite your history as if every high and low were perfectly offered to develop you into the person you are today. Retell the story line, coming to the present moment as the culmination of all your learning.

Reach Out

Get together with a loved one or a friend and go on a silent Venus scavenger hunt. Each of you should come back with six symbols of relationship happiness.

Drink some tea together and discuss your findings—in particular, discuss how your findings relate to your highest octave of love.

Risk It

Dare to tell someone how much you value them, without needing anything in return. Let them know why they matter to you so much and ask: "How may my love serve you?" The key is to offer this without consideration for reciprocity.

Reflect

Watch the following cinematic love stories, each of which illuminates different facets of romantic love:

- *Out of Africa*

- *Jerry Maguire*

- *A Star Is Born* (2018 version)

Discuss which character is most like you in love and why.

Talking Circle Questions

Gather with one or more people who have read this chapter. Using a talking piece everyone has agreed on (see note to "Talking Circle Questions" in chapter 2), have each person answer the following questions, one at a time. Make sure there is no cross-talk or side-talk; this is a time for completely undistracted, uninterrupted sharing. Before beginning, agree to keep what is said in the circle confidential, to listen deeply, to speak without rehearsing, and to be aware of time so that all have a chance to answer each question in the time available.

1. How do you most like to express love in intimate relationship?

2. How do you most like to have love expressed toward you in intimate relationship?

3. Do you feel best giving all your love to one intimate partner, or does it feel better to spread your love around? What challenges have come from whatever your propensity is?

4. Talk about your own Venus placement. Are you in Primitive, Adaptive, or Evolving space? What actions or internal shifts might help you in more skillful expression?

5. Go around the circle and have each person give appreciation to the person to their left. Be specific in mentioning the ways they *are* beautiful, balanced, and harmonious or the ways they *express* beauty, balance, and harmony.

Some day, after we have mastered the
winds, the waves, the tides and gravity,
we shall harness for God the energies
of love. Then for a second time
in the history of the world,
we will have discovered fire.

PIERRE TEILHARD DE CHARDIN

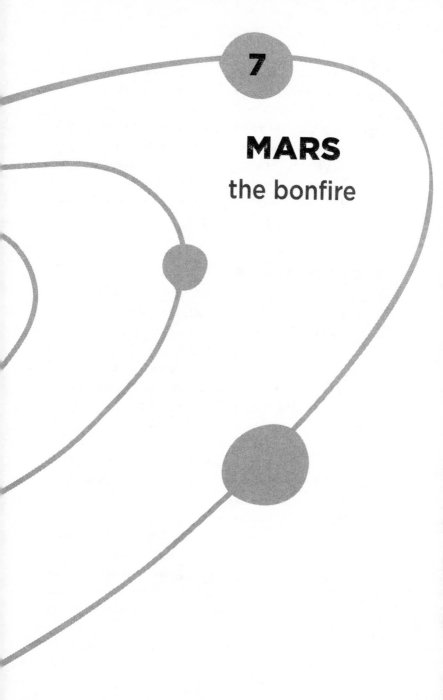

7

MARS

the bonfire

The archetype of Mars is about action, assertion, the masculine, and forward motion toward goals and accomplishments. It brings the courage and inspiration required to risk venturing beyond our comfort zones in order to achieve a higher good. In its more destructive expression, Mars brings impulses and drives toward aggression and war; in its constructive and positive expression, it inspires strong and sure action toward building a better world for ourselves and others.

THE MYTH OF MARS

Ancient Roman myth celebrated Mars as the god of war and as guardian of agriculture. The son of Jupiter and Juno (or, according to some versions of the story, of Juno only, through a form of immaculate conception involving a very special flower), Mars characterized virility and military might aimed toward a final goal of creating secure, safe peace. The wolf was a common symbol of Mars in Roman art and literature. Festivals in Mars's honor were held in his namesake month (Martius, or March), a time of year that was at the end of the farming season—an ideal time for launching military campaigns. Mars was believed to be the father of Romulus and Remus, the twin founders of Rome; the story goes that they were conceived when Mars raped a sleeping vestal virgin, Silvia.

A very important god in the Roman mythic tradition, Mars had many temples and altars built in his honor throughout the Roman Empire. Mars's Greek counterpart, Ares, was the namesake of the astrological sign Aries. Mars was considered to be a levelheaded defender of Roman borders and of the Roman way of life.

THE BONFIRE

A bonfire is a celebration of the illuminating, thrilling, inspiring, potentially dangerous element of fire. It represents the power of human beings to channel and use this resource for the good of all. In community gatherings, a bonfire symbolizes collective, hard-won effort. The bonfire reminds us that when we use the highest application of assertion, bravery, and excellence, our achievements surpass our individual quests and become of service to the collective good.

The sheer power and dynamism of the bonfire reminds everyone to act with courage and to reach for accomplishments that honor the interests and concerns of the community or collective. Seen this way, the archetype of Mars is about gathering the inner fire to conquer fears and actualize daring deeds on behalf of connected, collective evolution.

MARS IN THE SIGNS

The sign placement of Mars reveals the ways in which we express our force of will, wield our power, and get things done. It can also help us understand our tendencies toward aggression (or lack thereof) and the particular ways in which our libidos are expressed.

Mars in Aries

Mars in Aries can confer amazing energy and initiatory power. There are few placements better for getting things done. While it surely feels at home here, this placement can mean challenges with managing aggression and impulsivity. It could bring habits of restlessness, immaturity, a desire to *act* (possibly before thinking things through), and a tendency to charge ahead before others are ready to go along.

PRIMITIVE Oh, crap—you knocked another player down. Your guess? They deserved it. If it's not *your way*, why do it? You take what you want, when you want it. You really don't need anyone else's consent. What works best for you? Push, push, push . . . and then, mow down anyone or anything that hasn't taken the hint and gotten the heck out of your way!

ADAPTIVE You play hard for your team or on behalf of your cause. You apply your extensive energy toward raising the bar for yourself and others, and you can be counted on to take a hit for the team and to rise above the fray in a space of honor and courage.

Recognizing your tendency to charge ahead without consent from others, you apply some of your prodigious energy to making sure that everyone involved is okay with the direction things are going—*before* you make any decisions that will affect them. You even begin to find that your inner fires are stoked by others' assertiveness. You see that you do better within yourself when you join forces with others to create long-term fulfillment of a vision.

EVOLVING Your brave heart reflects the possibility of true, noble acts on behalf of community. The fire that burns strongly within you becomes a radiant signpost and source of energy for others, rather than a firestorm. People come to you to help them find their courage to do things they previously could not even imagine. Where others see intractable barriers to a sustainable and equitable community, you see a challenge worth taking. Your new motto: "All for one and one for all!"

Pat, with Mars in Aries, grew up in a military family in which aggression was seen as a core strength. He strove to excel in competitive sports. He was great at football and basketball, and he was a leader in his friend group, often ringleading risky adventures. He mocked and teased any peer who voiced caution or didn't want to go along with his tribe. This mode served him well throughout college, where he was a star athlete, and throughout his early years in the corporate world as a young professional, where he quickly battled his way to the top ranking on his sales team. His tough resoluteness cowed anyone who showed up with any amount of openness or uncertainty, and his financial success seemed to support his belief that vulnerability was a weakness.

Then he met Vanessa, a spirited young woman who came from a very different background. He was absolutely smitten with her, and she with him. But as they deepened their partnership and considered marriage, she began to insist that his "get out of my way so I can get this done my way" approach to life was not going to work for her. She felt subtly bullied and manipulated in ways she knew she couldn't tolerate long term; she knew it would not work for him to be the man with whom she would raise children.

With classic Mars in Aries energy, Pat threw himself into seeking ways to transform the conditioning he had received from his family. He fought tooth and nail to learn better relationship skills: to hear and value others and to manage his impulsivity and impatience when others needed to be heard. In the process of learning to be the man he wanted to be in his relationship, he recognized that the best use of his extraordinary physical power was to build things that mattered to other people. He became one of the chief construction leaders for Habitat for Humanity.

Mars in Taurus

Taurus grounds the forward-thrusting energy of Mars in earthy stillness. Its focus on material concerns and sensual pleasures can create stuck-ness, selfishness, and naysaying—a resistance to the momentum and action orientation of this archetype. Skillfully expressing this placement requires conscious focus on building one's will to act and create, rather than staying mired in the pleasures of the present moment. Once the Mars in Taurus individual truly sets their mind to something, their tenacity makes them unstoppable, and their levelness makes them hard to distract.

PRIMITIVE "No" is your first and last answer. You want to play in your own sandbox and not share with others. Where others push you, you double down with stubbornness and laziness. If anyone's looking for you, their best bet is to find you curled up on the couch eating crappy food and bingeing on reality shows.

ADAPTIVE Once you commit, it will be tough for anyone to find a more loyal champion of your cause. Your remarkable endurance means you're in it for the long haul. Nothing will deter you from helping others to go the distance. You possess a laudable sense of timing and pacing, and you are able to ensure that others feel relaxed in their efforts. As you work to realize a goal, you illuminate the beauty of earnest effort, sweating, and striving.

EVOLVING You are the rock from which all others spring forth into action. People know that you will hold down the fort so others can shine. Safety and security for all is your primary motivator; you are exquisitely capable of bringing everyone together in a heightened sense of harmony and purpose.

Mars in Gemini

In Gemini, the energy of Mars without a deep sense of overarching purpose and a highly structured big-picture plan can be diffused to a point of ineffectiveness. When skillfully expressed, this placement can bring the power of abstract ideas into concrete realization. With the fire of Mars, the mind of the writer and spokesperson can be highly developed in this placement.

PRIMITIVE How many moths can fly to a flame and get burned every time? As you run around in circles and create flash dances of chaos, you use your diffuse power to bring others into the chaos with you. Priorities? They want you to have priorities? They should know better! You have too many jelly beans spread out all over the floor, and they all look pretty to you. No one can make you choose. Now, gossip? That's something you can get behind. You spread it like the plague, especially when you know it will cause a shitstorm. There are few things you like better than creating one of those and then rolling around in the mess.

ADAPTIVE Your ability to work on multiple things at the same time recalls the skills of a master juggler; each shiny ball is attended to with equal care. You are true to each concern others may have. Your work ethic is impeccable because you recognize that every point of view and part is essential. Others come to you to joyfully problem-solve complexity and work toward a collaborative solution. Your walk is your talk; people feel elevated by the breezy, cool manner you effortlessly bring, even to a crisis.

EVOLVING Your words and actions match and invigorate those of others in their plans of implementation. People come to you to sort out priorities and bring out the best ideas for all. Your knowledge base is exceptional; what others don't know how to do, you quickly and thoroughly study so that you can be of skilled support. When others do important work with you, they know it will get done not only with great care but also with a burst of magic.

Nothing is too minor for you to willingly lend your support. You recognize how all parts of the puzzle—large and small—need to be attended to in order to fit together in the big picture.

Kyle's Mars is in Gemini. She started off her career as an advertising executive; she loved to travel and was especially good at selling multiple ideas on multiple platforms. Unfortunately, she was also known to be not that accurate with her promises or her pitches—she moved so quickly and mercurially that sometimes she was hasty and unrealistic.

Kyle decided to join a mindfulness program to learn how to quiet her overly active mind and restless body, which led her to transform her life and become a teacher of mindfulness practices to mothers of preschool students. She became known for her ability to quiet a room with very intentional movement and speech.

Mars in Cancer

When blended with the fiery directness of Mars, Cancer's watery emotionality, nurturing qualities, and receptivity provide either a balancing counterpoint or a soggy, frustrating mess. Skillful use of this placement requires special attention to emotion management and empathic sensitivity to the moods and mind-sets of others.

PRIMITIVE Like the preschooler who is still very alive inside you, you're not well inclined to anyone telling you "It's time to go!" when you don't feel like going. No one can make you! Your feelings are too overwhelming. You know there's stuff to do, but how can anyone expect you to get past these big, giant, heavy, hard-to-feel feelings? You'd much rather cry until someone takes care of *you*—while also taking care of whatever else needs taking care of. "I need my mommy!" is your constant subtext when things need to be done. "Stop pushing me to be an adult and handle things. I'll guilt trip you until I get my way."

ADAPTIVE You come to recognize that you are fully responsible for your actions. You begin to intentionally develop tools to practice managing your intense feelings. And you don't lose your sensitivity; you simply begin to use it to be sensitive to others' moods and to empathically inspire them to act with maturity. Your highly developed nurturing capacities urge others to collaborate and persevere through the most challenging circumstances or obstacles.

EVOLVING Divine Mother energy works through you in any endeavor in which you participate. Your heightened awareness of others' core needs allows you to motivate them from a deeply emotional place. Your accomplishments incentivize others, bringing social groups together on a universal basis of empathy and maturity. All you do, you do with profound gratitude for the gifts of life and the purpose of unity.

Mars in Leo

Fiery Mars and fiery Leo make a good match when it comes to big actions that make a big impact. Pitfalls with this placement can include forgetting that the task at hand isn't just about making the Mars in Leo person look spectacular. When the Mars in Leo person is able to remember and honor the needs and values of others as they make their big splash, they can be highly effective world changers, celebration makers, and creative problem solvers who never forget to bring the love and the fun.

PRIMITIVE "It's all for me, right? If I do this thing, I'll be the star, right? Even if I don't do much, I'll get the credit, as long as I show up and be my Most Show-Stopping Self, right?"

You're a glutton for activities that feature *you*; you don't really need for them to have any substance. You make sure everyone knows every little thing you do because you can't get enough praise. As soon as you receive it, its impact evaporates, leaving a vacuum you need to fill, posthaste. You'll do all you can to get more, even if it means torpedoing the whole project the Mars energy is driving you to accomplish.

ADAPTIVE Your heart is in everything you do. Others feel you as the supreme cheerleader, praising them and inviting them to play at the next level—whatever that level is for them. People count on you to bring joy to their projects. You see hard work as an opportunity to express the delight of achieving. Your "yes" to getting it done rings out like a bell of clarity and wonder, audible the world over. You move toward action from a place of *yes, we can!*

EVOLVING Childlike innocence and purity motivate you to help anyone you can. With you, others have a direct experience of love as the elbow grease of all creation. Your super-affectionate style of doing and interacting makes everyone feel included in events; all feel a joyful part of community building. Your work ethic shines, sparkling on others in a way that puts pep in their step.

LeAnn's Mars in Leo set her up to be a star. From day one, she was singing, dancing, and acting her life story. When she was cast in her first film at the age of eight, she was quickly overwhelmed with impersonal, fawning attention. She grew used to this treatment, and although it left her empty and craving more, she couldn't handle a day without it. Only after years of therapy did LeAnn realize she would never feel true love or joy through flattery from sycophants who did not really know her heart. She developed a strong personal practice incorporating creative writing, singing, and mindfulness, and she found a center within her that knew its own gifts without constant external validation.

LeAnn is still a successful entertainer; today, she chooses to work on artistic projects that lead from the heart, while leading others into their own radiance.

Mars in Virgo

The categorizing, organizing, detail-oriented principle of Virgo can be a great complement to the forward motion of Mars. Not many people can confidently, skillfully produce something beautiful or useful without a great deal of editing or tweaking;

with the Virgo lens, this is actually a possibility. When less skill is applied in expressing this placement, however, the need for perfection can set one up for a lack of forward motion; in this case, the Mars in Virgo person can stay mired in tiny details, judging themselves harshly while things fall apart around them.

PRIMITIVE You break everything you do into so many parts, you can't find what you are looking for. If you have to build a house, you might spend a year sorting tiny screws into individual compartments, unable to begin until everything is in its proper place.

You judge yourself and others mercilessly for how poorly things get done. You spool out endless martyr stories with yourself as the protagonist. "No one gets how hard I work at being petty and superior," you might say if you were to say the real, honest truth. Your contribution to the overall enterprise involves either hoarding or being a colossal mess.

ADAPTIVE You work to serve the collective without losing track of yourself. You are a specialist who can pinpoint the most effective way to get from A to Z. People can count on you to work hard and diligently without fanfare and to do what you need to do in terms of self-care so you can show up resourced. You see others' strengths and capacities and lead them to amplify their talents. Your own discipline is exemplary and provides others with a template for expressing greater discipline in their own lives.

EVOLVING Through you, others see a way through complex problems. You are able to get things done with no wasted motion and no complaints. People love working by your side; you know just how to enlist them in thoughtful progress. Your methods for unifying folks in a cause are time tested and sophisticated; you allow everyone to feel that their contributions are meaningful.

Mars in Libra

In Libra, the motivating energies of Mars have the potential to create balance, beauty, elegance, and harmony in whatever one does. The catch can be getting caught up in overconcern with appearances or having a tendency to hang back in indecision rather than act decisively. People with this placement have risen to be renowned mediators and diplomats.

PRIMITIVE You can hardly get anything done without checking your look in the nearest mirror or window glass. You can't seem to let go of your concern about how you look long enough to focus on getting things done. "Do I look good while doing it?" is the more important issue. "Does the mirror flatter me or make me look fat?"

Why should you choose one way when there are so many options? "Where do *you* want to go?" you ask whoever looks like they know what to do next. You don't have a will of your own; maybe you'll just follow them. Wherever you end up should be fine as long as you look good.

ADAPTIVE You excel at balancing work and play, and you show others how to do the same. Your understanding of the ways in which others operate allows all parties to realize their goals with calm confidence. Weighing out the best paths to the result is your forte, and you feel confident that together, you'll create a fulfilling outcome. People come to you to realize the most artistic and beautiful way to get things done.

EVOLVING Your motivation to serve the collective comes from a deep neutrality and patience. In all your actions, you foresee long-lasting consequences, which makes you especially gifted at temperate, wise decision-making. People gather around you to work on outstanding efforts of peace and art because they sense that in your guidance, all will proceed with a rich combination of gentleness and decisiveness.

Mars in Scorpio

This placement carries incredible potential for transformative action. The key to its skillful expression is to go beyond unhealthy obsessions and motivations and to use its prodigious power, insight, and strength of feeling to foment goodness and progress, rather than sinking into underwater depths of drama and self-punishing despair.

PRIMITIVE "Stash" is your middle name, and "stealth" is your code name. What you do is none of anyone else's business. The truth is, you're deeply ashamed of what you do; your experience of your internal self and its external expression is of a cauldron of misdeeds and rationalizations. No one need worry about your receiving your proper punishment; you punish yourself daily for your wicked behavior.

ADAPTIVE Fearless and intrepid, you actualize heroic feats with the support of like-minded others. You have no secrets to keep. Behind all you do is the cause of freeing people from ancestral shame and oppression. You gather yourself and others from the shadows to transform negative vibrations into healthy, lasting accomplishments.

You are willing to die for the cause, and yet, you take impeccable care of yourself and others so that all may live long and prosper.

EVOLVING   Like an eagle, you fly higher than the noise to bring perspective to all of the collective's steps and procedures. With you as a leader, folks are clued in to the eternal and repeating role of karma. The roads you all take together consider both the light and the dark; they do not deny anyone's pain or suffering. You guide with the knowledge that what you all create together has lasting implications for the Earth and the soul. You can be trusted to guard the vulnerable and inspire the invincible in all quests.

Mars in Sagittarius

The symbol for Sagittarius is a horizontal line with an arrow rising from it at a 45-degree angle, pointing to the right; this is a good illustration of the sign's propensity for movement both forward and upward. Mars in Sag people are able to do a lot with a great deal of fiery energy. However, they can get tripped up by a few less skillful Sagittarian habits: (1) partying a little too hard, (2) leaping before planning, or (3) some hotheadedly conceived combination of the two.

PRIMITIVE   You party hard, and then you tell people you partied even harder than you actually did. Why work when you can freeload off of others who want to be around you just to hear your exaggerations and tall tales? Bragging about something is better than really doing it, anyhow. Your ribald tales are delicious fodder for others' supplication. You flit and flap all over the place without landing anywhere—being in motion is a great way to avoid boring, stressful responsibilities.

ADAPTIVE   You come to recognize that freedom comes not from dodging responsibility but from right action; when you do things for the right reasons, everyone—including you—benefits. From a place of hard-won wisdom, you come to understand how many others have helped you get where you now find yourself. Taking all the credit for your successes feels worse than empty; the joy you feel with others as you strive purposefully together toward excellence is authentic. You realize that meaning comes from merit gained in the context of overcoming adversity, and you act accordingly.

EVOLVING   Higher education fuels your actions. Consideration for outcomes is equal to the thoughtfulness of the process. When you join with others, you all feel a great freedom in the ways you all get to the finish line. You bring vitality and radiance to community efforts because you see each person's truth in operation; you are able to nourish the capacities of others to authentically deliver in a space of contagious liberation.

Mars in Capricorn

The Mars in Capricorn native will tend to like things taken care of, handled, checked off, and worthy of praise. This placement sets one up to be responsible and productive in the present and able to plan well for the future. A steady climb up the mountain, with each footfall placed with care, is their style. Where the Mars in Capricorn person is less skillful, they might tend toward overwork, bossiness, lack of emotional investment or expression, or self-doubt. Social climbing can be another hazard of this ambitious placement.

PRIMITIVE Bossy and righteous is how you do things, so nobody had better get in your way. If there is a status symbol involved, you'll show up to pursue a goal; if not, everyone can count you out. You don't want to be bothered with real feelings about how the collective is getting from point A to point B because you only know one feeling: the feeling of being right. Your operating manual is set to robotic.

If you can control the outcome, you will, at all costs—even if it means deceiving others and yourself over and over again.

ADAPTIVE You are the epitome of collaborative, nonauthoritarian leadership. Your motivation to achieve comes from a mountain of compassion and valuing of the inclusion of all voices. You come to recognize that no one wins unless all feel recognized and worthy and that excellence comes from solid self-approval, not accolades from others. Your greatest pride comes from helping others who have less than you; you no longer seek acknowledgment for that service because you find true satisfaction in giving.

EVOLVING All who wish to be embraced by a true master of mind, spirit, feeling, soul, and body come to you. Your realization of what truly matters engages you in social causes that steadily and consistently generate outcomes of inspiration, and you always make sure that everyone involved gets credit for those outcomes. People who work with you consistently comment on how you motivate by humble example and how you illustrate the importance of right action through daily kindness, acted upon deliberately. You no longer feel divided between a public and private self; your transparency is the same, no matter where you find yourself.

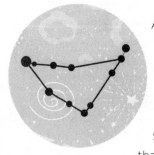

Alison, with her Mars in Capricorn, comes from a family of rock climbers who spent lots of time on climbing walls, camping trips, and day hikes. From an early age, she learned that life was about surmounting obstacles. She loved climbing and trained harder than anyone else, always trying to find that next peak of achievement. By the age of thirty, she needed a knee replacement and came to recognize that the stress on her joints was mirrored by the mental and emotional stress of relentlessly pushing herself.

Alison began to understand that the point of the journey was the journey, not the destination; she learned to relax in the joy of the process of manifesting, instead of constantly looking for the next horizon. She developed a line of women's outdoor clothing that emphasizes comfort, care, and ease—a brand that expresses her recognition of the importance of taking great care of the body that is pushed to the limits of its strength and stamina.

Mars in Aquarius

In Aquarius, independence, headiness, and originality color the expression of the Mars archetype. Its most skillful expression comes through as the powerful reforming and reinvention of norms that no longer serve; as the willingness to be fully one's self and to let others be *them*selves, while still working harmoniously together toward a valuable goal. Less skillful Mars in Aquarius traits can come through as pushiness, superiority, or dismissing of others' efforts.

PRIMITIVE You move weirdly, oddly out of orbit. Your mojo is tied to rebellion in such a way that mere human goals are beneath you. If others challenge your way of doing things, they don't need to worry about stress; you'll just quit or cause so much upheaval that everyone will forget why they all came together in the first place. You *are* the beat of a different drummer; you don't particularly care what anyone else's beat is.

ADAPTIVE Your jet engine runs on noble ideals and in bringing folks of all kinds together. Your focus is like a laser; you stay the course, despite personal doubts or inconveniences. Those who work with you and your teammates will be elevated to their best selves and will feel embedded in principles of equality and unity.

EVOLVING You are a true catalyst for positive social change. Everyone feels included in your lofty ambitions for the world; they know they are welcome in the world of doing on behalf of the greater good. With you, people see no divisions or walls, only the possibility of the Age of Aquarius—a world of abundance, where every being and creature has enough of all it needs.

Mars in Pisces

A person with Mars in Pisces is great at going with the flow of life but can be troubled by difficulty in knowing what they want or how to get it. Anger and assertiveness don't come naturally to this placement; they are more likely to have trouble choosing a direction and sticking with it. Creative expression is important here, and any issues that galvanize the Mars in Pisces person enough to get them to take a true stand are likely to have something to do with dissolving obstacles to love and connection.

PRIMITIVE "Who, me, a victim?" you ask. Well, no matter what you try to do, *someone* is not understanding your rhythms and circuitry, and it's just not worth the effort to get people to accept you where you are. Moving along a highway of rushing water is terribly difficult! So, you might as well just float along and let things happen. If things get too tough, there is always your favorite action: escape through any means possible.

ADAPTIVE Empathy guides your every action. Your attunement to every living thing provides you with the core impetus to stay on track and deliver on promises you have made. People love to work with you; in your presence, they feel the incredible glow of being seen in their highest incarnation. Your egoless efforts inspire others to be noble and passionate about generous, full-hearted giving.

EVOLVING Psychic, guided by spirit, you channel the highest vibrations for every step that you and your community take. Others are astounded by your ability to move energy in service of miracles. When you and others join together to do something, all involved feel as though they are on a magic carpet ride imbued with unlimited possibility and fulfillment.

Practices for Mars • • • • • • • • • • •

Dive In

Pick something to do each day for a week that you have never done before in your life. Read the Evolving description of your Mars; see how much of that energy you can bring to the way you do this new thing.

Also, choose one thing you have *avoided* doing that needs completion. Ask two people you know to be your support squad. Set a date to complete the task; then plan a celebration for yourself when you cross the finish line.

Risk It

Decide to learn one new, difficult activity: a sport, game, or practice that you would be thrilled to accomplish and that will strengthen your body. Ask one person to join you in learning this new Mars activity. Push your edge of learning and pay close attention to the cues of your body. Don't override your limits; guard your safety and health.

Reach Out

Think of someone in your life who could really use your sweat and time to get something accomplished. Make it a doable and timely endeavor, where you can offer your assistance and see it through.

Also, let someone else know about something you are struggling to complete; ask them to help you navigate your resistance and create a new strategy for approaching this goal.

And finally, sometimes, in our unskilled Mars iterations, we do something that causes harm to someone else. Dare to admit where your actions and behaviors have caused others stress or harm and offer a repair. Write a note with the following steps to those affected by your actions:

1. I did _____. (No explanations or excuses; just full accountability.)

2. That behavior probably felt _____ to you.

3. What can I do to make up for the hurt I caused you? Please let me know in person or with a reply to this letter.

Reflect

Write a list of your five key accomplishments of the past ten years, but do so from the perspective of your ten-years-older-than-you-are-now self. Note what these key achievements are and how you imagine it felt to climb that mountain. Who or what assisted you along the way?

Create a contract with yourself to do the five things you listed. Sign it.

Talking Circle Questions

Gather with one or more people who have read this chapter. Using a talking piece everyone has agreed on (see note to "Talking Circle Questions" in chapter 2), have everyone answer the following questions, one at a time. Make sure there is no cross-talk or side-talk; this is a time for completely undistracted, uninterrupted sharing. Before beginning, agree to keep what is said in the circle confidential, to listen deeply, to speak without rehearsing, and to be aware of time so that all have a chance to answer each question in the time available.

1. Share three of your biggest achievements and two of your biggest failures. Describe what you learned from both.

2. What have you helped others do that they couldn't have done without you?

3. What motivates you the most to act for the highest good? How can you stoke that fire more regularly?

4. What personal self-sabotaging behaviors do you most struggle with? Why?

5. Name two people you admire most for how they do things. Why?

6. No matter what shape you are in, name three ways your body is your ally.

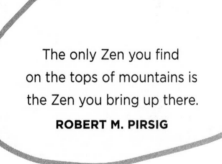

The only Zen you find
on the tops of mountains is
the Zen you bring up there.

ROBERT M. PIRSIG

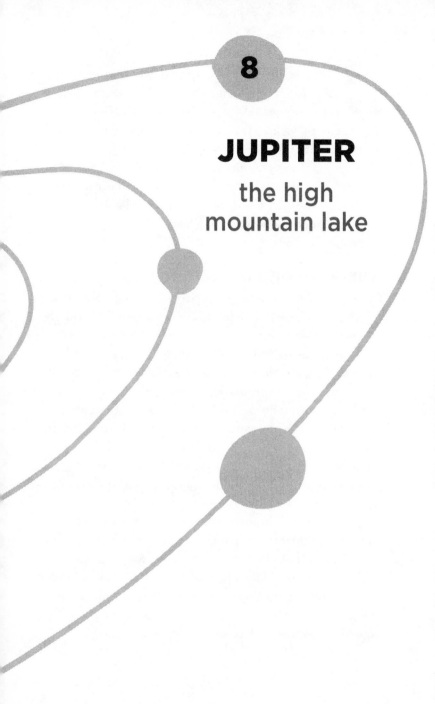

8

JUPITER
the high mountain lake

Jupiter is the archetype of expansion, growth, and optimism. In the lexicon of astrology, Jupiter governs generosity, abundance, success, and luck. In particular, Jupiter governs higher learning and the philosophical and moral principles that it embraces, as well as the learning one does through travel and exposure to other ways of life. Unchecked and excessive Jupiter energy can bring overindulgence, over-reaching, a focus on wealth and status over what is good and right and true, and excessive confidence.

THE MYTH OF JUPITER

The name of the Roman god Jupiter—the equivalent of the Greek god Zeus—is made from Latin word roots that roughly translate to "sky father."

Jupiter is the Roman god of the sky and of thunder and the king of the gods. He was one of several children his mother, Ops, had with the then-king of the gods, Saturn; Saturn began to swallow his own offspring because of rumors that one of them would eventually overthrow him. After Saturn had swallowed Neptune, Pluto, Ceres, Juno, and Vesta, Ops thought better of handing over her newest baby; she gave birth to Jupiter secretly and then handed Saturn a swaddled rock, which he ate instead.

Jupiter fulfilled Saturn's worst fears by overthrowing the old king as punishment for having eaten all of Jupiter's siblings. Once he had grown into manhood, Jupiter forced his father to regurgitate all the children he'd swallowed, and they all joined together to wrest rulership from Saturn. They decided to divide the universe into three parts: the underworld for Pluto, the heavens for Jupiter, and the sea for Neptune.

THE HIGH MOUNTAIN LAKE

Few sights are more refreshing and inspiring than a pure, fresh-water lake high in the mountains; few scents and sensations can match the unending expansiveness of the air and the atmosphere in such a setting. The high mountain lake symbolizes ascent, clarity, reflection, and celebration.

Aspiring toward Evolving expressions of Jupiter brings this same sense of unlimited and sacred connectedness to higher vibrations of meaning and transcendence. When the most valorous expression of Jupiter's placement in your chart is achieved, you reach a pinnacle of purity and higher wisdom.

JUPITER IN THE SIGNS

The sign placement of Jupiter gives valuable insights about capacity for and ways of expressing optimism, expansion, growth, abundance, higher learning, and success.

Jupiter in Aries

Jupiter expands and intensifies whatever it touches; with a placement in Aries, this expansion affects the skillful energies of bravery, determination, willingness to risk, spiritedness, and commitment to forward movement—*and* the less skillful energies of impulsivity, unhealthy risk taking, selfishness, and immaturity.

PRIMITIVE Talk about inflated! They might as well blow you up into a blimp of self-congratulation. Striking out into new territory is your jam, and it doesn't matter who you pummel to get there. Someone wants to walk with you? They can try, but they'll just be left in the dust.

ADAPTIVE   Your stamina for serving others has no bounds. The vibrant, constant energy you possess goes toward feats of kindness for your beloveds. Reaching for the summit is no problem with you; if needed, you will carry others on your back.

EVOLVING   Moral courage defines you. Through you, others see the possibility of noble miracles. No obstacle or skeptic can shut down your dedication to quality interactions and results. Others rely on you to be a tower of fortitude in rough times and a pinnacle of illumination in joyous times.

From an early age, Layla—with her Jupiter in Aries—was the most skillful, explosive soccer player on the field. She received tremendous rewards and honors for being the top scorer on every team she played with, and she was lovingly known for the temper tantrums she threw whenever she missed a goal. As Layla was practicing for the US Soccer National Amateur Cup, she blew out her knee and was laid up for six months.

During this time, Layla had to come to terms with having based her entire identity on being a superior athlete. While she was recuperating, she was offered an opportunity to work with the Special Olympics. In helping young people who had true adversities and difficulties, Layla discovered a sense of purpose and meaning. She eventually became the chair of the Special Olympics in her area and is known more for her exceptional service, dedication, and self-sacrifice than for her athletic mastery.

Jupiter in Taurus

In Taurus, Jupiter has the potential to expand one's grounded-ness and steadiness. This placement is a perfect setup for slow, steady, focused intention and work that follows the Earth's rhythms. However, less skillful expression can be a setup for laziness and stubborn intractability, as well as a preoccupation with material possessions and ownership.

PRIMITIVE   No one can lay around in splendor better than you! Too much of everything? Perfect! You don't want those underlings to share with you—you somehow know that you have been imperially chosen. Others should just relax and serve your pleasures.

ADAPTIVE   Your conservation of beauty and resources is not only generous but also well designed. You understand the long-term value of cultivating art and tending to the Earth. With you, others come to see the vast importance of preserving the natural wonders of this planet.

EVOLVING   You lead with grace and composure. Others are amazed at your patience and elegance when hosting a cause or event. You use your own resources to benefit the community, and you hold deep values of charity as your guide. With you, people feel grounded in taking a stand for an expanded love of nature and the body.

Jupiter in Gemini

With Jupiter in Gemini, mental and communicative activities are augmented, making this placement an ideal setup for con-versation and communication across all kinds of boundaries.

Unskillful expression can mean excessive distractibility and lack of organization, dissipating the placement's potential into a windy whorl that never quite condenses into anything tangible.

PRIMITIVE You have papers everywhere. You can't see your way through all your piles of stuff. Flitting everywhere and getting nothing done is your specialty. Like a hummingbird with ADHD, you fly in circles until you wear yourself out.

ADAPTIVE You are a stream of connected ideas; you are adept at networking for the best outcomes. Your mind works like a knitter, bringing folks together to share talents and knowledge. People come to you to brainstorm and strategize the most effective, coherent ways of approaching any problem.

EVOLVING Your alacrity in conversation and deliverables is unsurpassed. Groups circle around you for counsel on ethics and inclusivity. Words are sacred to you, and you are known for inspired and kind speech. There is no way to block you from conceiving new ideas and creating breakthrough inventions. *Can't* is not in your vocabulary.

Jupiter in Cancer

Here, Cancer's maternal, deeply feeling qualities can manifest as great love, kindness, and empathy—or as great neediness and a retreat into childlike expectations of being the center of everyone's nurturing attention.

PRIMITIVE You are a globe of feelings! They tumble out of you in all directions. You have not figured out how to grow up, but that's not a problem because being grown up seems pretty boring anyway. Those who lift you onto their laps and feed you will find you are the biggest and best baby. Chores? You? Don't ask—parents are supposed to handle that stuff!

ADAPTIVE   Your enlarged sense of responsiveness to all people allows you to embrace the most sensitive, complex issues with others with true emotional balance. You are keenly aware of how every nuance of a challenge is a prompt for subtle and appreciative inquiry. With you, others feel both nurtured and steadied to meet the demands of life in a graceful way.

EVOLVING   Your capacious and expansive energy surrounds all with a true feeling of rapture and motivation. Through you, others see the possibility of divine love in all matters, big and small. When there are impasses, you guide others to a place of genuine curiosity for resolution and communion. You come to see differences as simply opportunities to create more bridges of consciousness.

Cynthia has Jupiter in Cancer. She became accidentally pregnant at age sixteen and went on to have the child. The father did not stick around; by the time Cynthia was eighteen, she had met a dedicated partner, Rafael, and they married. She had two more children by the time she was twenty-three. She prided herself on being an incredibly devoted and capable mother and found other young mothers to join with and receive support from.

When she turned twenty-nine, Cynthia realized she had deferred all her dreams of self-development in favor of her children. She returned to school to become a school counselor, discovering her own extraordinary capacity to mother and care for other children and to achieve her own dreams and goals.

Jupiter in Leo

The creative, playful, expressive heart of Leo loves to be abundantly demonstrative and joyful, and Jupiter can take this to the next level! Giving in to cravings to want to be lifted up and celebrated at the individual level can mean less skillful expression here.

PRIMITIVE You surround yourself with sycophants and relish the limelight in any way you can. You never feel that enough time has been taken to talk about *you*. The full meaning of *diva/divo* can be best understood by the one who has the pleasure of spending time in your glowing sphere of influence.

ADAPTIVE Love radiates from you, shining throughout the whole room, dropping a light coating of glimmering acceptance dust on everything. Others bask in your inspired appraisal of them. That song "Ain't no mountain high enough/ Ain't no valley low enough/Ain't no river wide enough/to keep me away from you, babe"? You may as well have written it.

EVOLVING Your capacity to inject joy into any endeavor is phenomenal. You guide others to their bliss not only through pleasure but also through their contributions to others. Your optimism is contagious and reliable.

Jupiter in Virgo

As it magnifies discipline, organization, responsibility, responsiveness, and careful decision-making, Jupiter in Virgo is a setup for effective planning and follow-through. This placement can also bury effective outward action in overattention to details, nitpicky criticism of others, and self-critical downward spirals.

PRIMITIVE You demonstrate incredible ease in exaggerating what's wrong. Any flaw you detect in yourself or others, you highlight with a neon pen. When in doubt—and that's most of the time—you become petty and critical. This prevents others from finding out how terribly inadequate you are. How could anyone possibly do anything right in your company?

ADAPTIVE You begin to see the world's perfect weave, which includes all imperfections and which allows for humble mistakes. You learn to bring people together based on divine order and expected fallibility. When you assess a situation, you look at it from a place of neutral and helpful curiosity.

EVOLVING Service with a true grin is your specialty. Your ability to see what is needed and attend to it without drama is remarkable. Others feel profoundly understood in your company, encouraged to bring their "A game" without perfectionism. Helping is your true nature, and you bring that help to others while holding great respect for their own capacities to be of assistance.

Jupiter in Libra

This placement holds potential for cultivation of peace and harmony on a grand scale—or an overfocus on shallower concerns around appearances and social climbing.

PRIMITIVE   You are a specialist in vanity, superficiality, and ambivalence. Comparing is your way of connecting. "Who is more attractive than me?" is your most important consideration. You're a social butterfly with catty cat claws, ready to poke holes in others to make yourself look better.

ADAPTIVE   Quintessentially fair and balanced, you are a conveyer of peaceful options. People are drawn to your ease and comfort with beauty and depth. You calmly and cooly hold space for difficult topics and issues. Temperance is your gift to others.

EVOLVING   You perch upon a multicolored tree branch of understanding; folks feel seasoned compassion when you hear and hold them. Your aesthetics of communication and your ways of getting things done are uniquely fresh and engaging. No one feels left out in your company; everyone can find a beautiful way to be themselves and be honored around you.

Growing up, Mario—who has Jupiter in Libra—received constant attention for his sexy charm and good looks. He spent the first ten years of his dating life popping in and out of bed with glamorous models and superstars. He had a very easy, pleasure-filled life, and he knew it—until his best friend died in a drunk-driving crash. Mario went to a very dark place and reemerged knowing that his running around didn't offer him any true comfort or depth when it came to facing life's real issues.

At this time, Mario met a young man who had had his face scarred and burned while serving in Iraq.

Mario became interested in helping people with facial deformities get the surgeries they needed through donated services from plastic surgeons. He now leads an organization that connects charitable plastic surgeons with those who most need their services.

Jupiter in Scorpio

Expanding Scorpio's secrecy, jealousy, and attraction to the underworld can bring incredible challenges. Magnifying the emotional intensity, empathic ability, and laser focus of Scorpio can bring incredible gifts. Which shark will you feed?

PRIMITIVE With you, dancing in the dark takes on new dimensions. Walking the edge comes with razors and rage. Sex, drugs, and rock and roll find their wild side in you. Nothing is too ghastly for you to consider. As an emotional vampire, you know just how to suck out the life force of others.

ADAPTIVE Transformative acumen is your skill. If *anyone* can compost the negative and turn it into meaningful positives, you can. People come to you with their most grueling pain because they know you can feel it with them and help them toward post-traumatic growth.

EVOLVING You are the meeting place for enormous generative growth. People come to work with you to act and interact in the context of great and noble ideas and to be reminded that the impossible can become doable with the support of unwavering conviction. Soulful, profound insights are your specialty—and for you, they come through a humble channeling of the ancients.

Jupiter in Sagittarius

Jupiter is the ruling planet of Sagittarius, whose energy already tends toward the expansive (when skillful) or toward the excessive (when unskillful). Augmented by the Jupiter archetype, this placement can predispose one toward grandiosity and partying until they drop or, when its bigness is entrained within higher learning, teaching, knowledge, optimism, and mastery, toward great achievement in support of the collective.

PRIMITIVE For you, bigger is better, and more is never enough. You enlarge, exaggerate, propagate, and take no responsibility for overreaching. "Go excessive or go home" is your motto. Hangovers—both emotional and substance related—are your frequent companions.

ADAPTIVE You are the world's best cheerleader. With you, others feel contagious optimism; they know in their hearts and bodies that together, you can accomplish anything you set your collective mind to. Honesty and authenticity are your calling cards; knowledge is what you consistently seek. You possess a measured joy founded in gratitude and stability.

EVOLVING Mind, body, and spirit are integrated within you; you use the collective energies to heal yourself and others. You have studied and gained mastery in many areas of knowledge so that you can educate and engage your community. People trust your unimpeachable ethics and standards and feel an unbridled joy in your affectionate company.

Jupiter in Capricorn

Expanding responsibility, forward thinking, perspective taking *or* expanding defensiveness, endless craving for and seeking of recognition, and an overconcern about reputation: these are the potentials and the possible liabilities of Jupiter in Capricorn.

PRIMITIVE You wield the sword of defensiveness better than anyone. Your cold austerity is unmatched, and your superior ways are unparalleled. You are above rules and regulations; you relentlessly seek recognition.

ADAPTIVE Your reputation is built on how many people you have assisted in reaching their goals. You humbly offer your wealth of mastery and experience to benefit the least advantaged. Working tirelessly on behalf of a lasting social cause gives you great joy and satisfaction.

EVOLVING You are a stand for seven generations of cause and effect: you recognize the impact others' choices have had for the generations before you, and you foresee the future impacts of those living now. This trait gives your leadership a perspective that is grounded in allowing people to see the long-term effects of all decisions, which impels others to make choices that promote sustainability. People come to work with you because they know your plans are credible. You are just as invested in living an emotionally fulfilling life as you are in realizing external goals.

Donald, whose Jupiter is in Capricorn, was raised in a family of businesspeople in which all were judged by their corporate performance and success. After earning an MBA at the University of Pennsylvania, he began his career in banking, quickly rising to a commanding

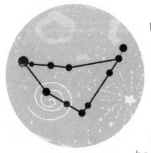

position in a world bank. At age thirty-three, he was brought down by a corruption scandal that involved the falsifying of business reports.

During his two-year stay in a white-collar prison, Donald realized that his preoccupation with wealth and power had robbed him of tender and vulnerable relationships with other human beings. He created a twelve-step program for people who have fallen into an addictive relationship with greed. Since that time, this program has helped many people find their way from greed to generosity.

Jupiter in Aquarius

The Aquarian celebration of uniqueness, big-picture thinking, and communitarian values goes big with Jupiter in play. So, too, can an overemphasis on difference for difference's sake or a stuck, know-it-all attitude that can come with thinking that one's own notion of the big picture is the *only* notion anyone should have.

PRIMITIVE Freak flags fly here! You're as weird, different, and nonconforming as possible, just because it gets people so excited and reactive. If others say "yes," you say "no." At the same time, you expect others to unquestioningly worship at the altar of your knowing. "If I believe it, you'd better, too"—that's your litmus test for the humans you'll accept into your circle.

ADAPTIVE You gather friends from all corners to create a feast of community. People come to you for support in thinking outside the box and sometimes in getting rid of the boxes altogether. Your vision is vast and practical, while also attending to unique, personal vantage points.

EVOLVING   You recognize that the future is ours if we all join together in our most vulnerable humanity, and your intention is to guide all those you can toward building a better world. You seek to achieve this by linking all strengths together. Recognizing that uncertainty is an incontrovertible reality, you honor not-knowing as a mystery to be lived.

Jupiter in Pisces

Here, Pisces's powerful capacities for empathy, psychic connectedness, and compassion expand. So, too, can the sense of dream time, of being lost, or of being a victim of one's circumstances or of other people.

PRIMITIVE   Sloshing around in confusion and avoidance is your calling card. Dreaming but not doing is your thing—so nobody had better ask you to follow through. If you haven't done something, it's definitely someone else's fault.

ADAPTIVE   Sensitively and artistically, you motivate others to wake to their dreams and do the work they need to do in order to realize them. People recognize your psychic gifts and consult with you for oracular guidance. Within you is a burning, active faith that leads others to great deeds.

EVOLVING   As a practical mystic, you galvanize miracles of cooperation and commitment. People come to you from all over to feel heartened in their hopes for humankind. Within you is an everlasting candle of empathy, kindness, and service.

Practices for Jupiter • • • • • • • • • •

Dive In

Using the Evolving definition of your Jupiter, do one thing a day that reaches for this octave of expression. Whatever you are able to do, record in a notebook entitled "Miracles Can Happen."

Reach Out

Write a definition of what generosity means to you and what would be your ultimate and realistic daily expression of generosity.

Practice that expression every day for one week.

Risk It

Jupiter asks us to expand our knowledge base, to become worldlier. Do its bidding by acquiring knowledge in an area you know nothing about. Pick anything you have been curious about but have not yet carved out the time or dedicated the energy to learn beyond the surface.

Spend a month studying this topic in one way or another to enhance your scope of abundance.

Reflect

When in your life have you felt, even for a moment, truly abundant and full of grace? Reflect on all the components of that moment or time. Gather materials that bring it to life for you now: photos, glitter, small objects—anything that brings that moment back for you as a felt experience.

Assemble your materials into a collage reflecting all the elements of that Jupiter experience. Share it with someone who cares about you.

Talking Circle Questions

Gather with one or more people who have read this chapter. Using a talking piece everyone has agreed on (see note to "Talking Circle Questions" in chapter 2), have each person answer the following questions, one at a time. Make sure there is no cross-talk or side-talk; this is a time for completely undistracted, uninterrupted sharing. Before beginning, agree to keep what is said in the circle confidential, to listen deeply, to speak without rehearsing, and to be aware of time so that all have a chance to answer each question in the time available.

1. Describe, in detail, what expands your senses of grace and gratitude.

2. Who has demonstrated a truly generous spirit to you? How?

3. Where do you tend to go overboard and become excessive? What triggers this?

4. When have you felt like you are truly learning? What is your best way to seek knowledge?

5. Tell people in this circle how they can support you to expand your sense of adventure and learning.

6. Have each person share one way this listening circle has extended their commitment to personal growth.

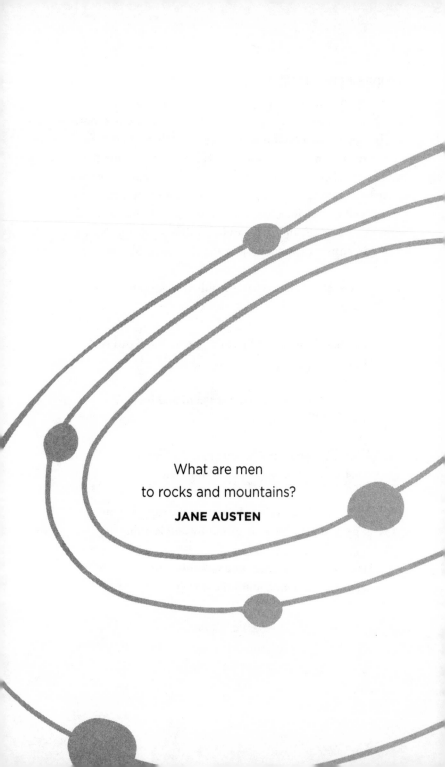

What are men
to rocks and mountains?

JANE AUSTEN

9

SATURN

the mountain

Saturn is limitation, tradition, necessity, structure, responsibility; it is what makes form from formlessness. It balances the expansive energy of Jupiter with contraction. This planet is a tough taskmaster, bringing us face to face with death, aging, and other cold, hard, concrete realities. Saturn separates us from the formless bliss from which we came. It represents Father Time and rules karma and justice. And although he might not be the first guy you'd invite to a dinner party, his strength, form, and structure are what make everything else possible.

THE MYTH OF SATURN

In ancient Roman mythology, Saturn was a god who oversaw agriculture and the seasons and was considered the father of the gods—one of the seven Titans eventually deposed by Jupiter, the son he never got a chance to eat (remember that the mother of Saturn's children handed him a rock instead, allowing Jupiter to escape and eventually overthrow him). Saturn's Greek counterpart was Kronos, the god who oversaw the passage of clock time. Temples and sacrifices dedicated to Saturn were a major part of Roman religious life; if Saturn wasn't on your side, your affairs were not likely to go well.

Saturnalia, an ancient Roman festival that was observed for seven days in December, was the most popular of all the Roman festivals. Saturday is named after Saturn.

THE MOUNTAIN

When we envision Saturn as a mountain, we are reminded that every one of us has incarnated to take the great climb of manifestation and completion of karma. On the great mountain, we endure the trials and tribulations of being human and face both our capacities and our limits. No one finishes the climb in a lifetime, but they do reach summits and peaks—and plummet to valleys, too.

We all have lessons to learn, and the importance of Saturn is in the learning of these lessons. We are all here to work through tremendous suffering to attain the solidity and peacefulness of the mountain. When we take up the work with humility and diligence—and without whining or self-pity—we can find great, lasting satisfaction in our self-development and in the deeds we do on behalf of all beings.

SATURN IN THE SIGNS

Saturn's placement in the birth chart is of vital importance to the big picture of each person's "life school" and powers of manifestation. It relays information about one's capacity for discipline, responsibility, rigor, and careful, persistent effort.

Saturn in Aries

Saturn in Aries can be expressed through commanding, dominating, and tyrannical tendencies. Its skillful expression is best seen in a protective, valorous, compassionate stance on behalf of others' well-being.

PRIMITIVE   Rash and hostile, you rule others' every move. You consider it your job to hurt others because, ultimately, it's for their own good. When you lift your hand, others had better jump; you have no time to consider anything else about them because your will must be done.

ADAPTIVE You use your considerable power and authority to serve the marginalized, you apply your bravery in support of those who cannot defend themselves, and you offer your strength of conviction and character as you work alongside others with gratitude.

EVOLVING You are a force of genuine kindness, rooted in deep empathy. You have understood cause and effect deeply, and you apply all your actions with thoughtful consideration. People say you are a hero for the underdog, but actually, you are working on saving your own soul by releasing your ego every day.

Saturn in Taurus

With the power of Saturn grounded into the earthy steadiness of Taurus, there can be a need for security and stability and for a gradual, long-term approach. It can be tempting to get completely stuck in stubbornness or in an overfocus on financial security. Skillfully expressed, Saturn in Taurus can bring great patience in the face of obstacles.

PRIMITIVE You are stuck like mud to a shoe; you won't budge. You are resentful and contemptuous, and you constantly feel cheated. You lord over others, withholding your time and energy in response to your perception that they are undervaluing you.

ADAPTIVE You accomplish things smoothly and consistently. You make sure to follow through on your word; you do not let petty feelings or heavy obstacles dissuade you from your path. Others remark on your centered way of doing things.

EVOLVING   You are like a Buddha in terms of your equanimity in attending to earthly matters. People flock to you to be part of your divine manifestation because your air of compassion is palpable. Your loyalty is undaunted for the awakening nature of all beings.

From a young age, Martha—with her Saturn in Taurus—loved fine things. She collected statues and jewelry and became obsessed with the television program *The Bachelor*—a show that fed her fantasies about finding a rich husband who would provide her with all the goodies she wanted and a lifetime of extravagant comfort.

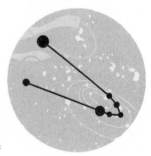

Her dreams seemed to come true when, in her twenty-fourth year, she found Brett: he was handsome, wealthy, and incredibly romantic. After two years of marital bliss and the arrival of their first child, Brett became more and more distant. Through a friend, Martha discovered that Brett had another wife and other children in another country where he traveled for business.

Martha had to come face to face with her shadow, which was that romantic ideals and security had clouded her own sense of values and self-esteem. She left her marriage and spent the next four years in committed therapy. She returned to school to study cosmetology and now volunteers as a mentor who teaches young women about the importance of agency and self-sufficiency.

Saturn in Gemini

People with this placement are highly adaptable and good at creating structure in the realm of mental abstraction. Less skillful expression can reveal itself as challenges with verbal expression and distractibility.

PRIMITIVE   Because you won't do the work required to learn to communicate effectively, you are stunted in your verbal skills. You use words carelessly and harmfully and with bravado, not caring what others think. Your mind is filled with constant noise, which you feed with more and more distractions—fulfilling your own deepest fear, which is that you will come across to others as stupid.

ADAPTIVE   Your attention to right speech is constant. You see words as heavenly tools for illumination. Wit and humor carry you into the world of connection. You always leave people feeling better about themselves. When you work beside others, they feel as though they could be quickly transported to their best possible mental state.

EVOLVING   Your clarity of thought and your understanding are remarkable. You are able to see through quagmires of confusion, and you help others see their own keys to decisive action. When people work with you, they are propelled into a visionary state of manifestation. In your case, if it can be said, it can be done.

Saturn in Cancer

Unskillful expression of the structure and discipline of Saturn through the emotional, maternal lens of Cancer might mean the feeling self's taking the reins without adequate support from reason and forethought. Skillfully worked with, however, this placement can support the realization of the best possible combination of nurturing compassion and solid boundaries—the ultimate in emotional intelligence.

PRIMITIVE Your feelings dictate the day. Moody and grumpy, you drag around like a cat with a big, wet tail. If you do not complete something, it is easy to blame others—after all, *they* made *you* feel bad. You won't take responsibility for your mistakes; you should get a pass anyway. Your parents are at fault for your whole lifetime of troubles.

ADAPTIVE You are acutely aware of the soft underbellies of others, and you protect their sensitivities through mindfulness and respectful behavior. People like to work beside you because they can rely on your ongoing nurturing and secure boundaries. Your reflective, calm nature supports others to settle into their competencies.

EVOLVING The wellspring of kindness emitting from you fills everyone around you. Manifesting your dreams comes through daily discipline and gentleness. Others love to be with you as you exude a grace of faith based on doing loving things consistently.

Saturn in Leo

The person with Saturn in Leo has the potential to lead and teach others with courage, creativity, and plenty of positive energy. Less skillfully expressed, this placement can come through as arrogant, self-centered, overly prideful, or attention-hungry.

PRIMITIVE You lead by navel gazing. If you want to do something, then everyone else should want to do it, too. You are so wrapped up in your own version of reality that you believe you should be given your very own reality show! Others find you to be insufferably self-obsessed.

ADAPTIVE You concentrate on heart-centered actions. People love to work beside you because you bring joy to the simplest of tasks. If you encounter someone who might be your archenemy, you find ways to make them your ally by cultivating their creative contribution.

EVOLVING Your expansive loving-kindness embraces all you do. Your motto is "if it isn't coming from the heart, it won't be done well." You are a stand for each unique, creative spark in a garland of expressive lights.

Priscilla, who has Saturn in Leo, grew up excelling in the dramatic arts. Known for her humor and comedic repartee, as well as her ability to entertain on the spot, she became popular in every circle she was part of. She could be counted on to show up as the life of the party. She worked hard on her own comedy improv act, and by the time she was eighteen she had become a featured player at a prominent comedy club in Chicago.

Priscilla went on to be a consistent, shining light in the world of improv comedy, logging dozens of years and hundreds of hours of hard work in this chosen vocation. What's most remarkable about her, however, is that she spends a good deal of time and effort helping other young comedians find their way to the spotlight.

Saturn in Virgo

In less skillful expressions, Saturn in Virgo can show up as intimidating in its hyper-focus on details and criticism of self and others. Fun and flexibility can seem out of reach. A more skillful use of this placement means learning to remember spaciousness, mindfulness, and self-care, while preserving enough rigor to get the important details right.

PRIMITIVE   Caught up in busyness like an ant wandering through piles of dirt, you cannot find any rest. You are duty-bound. Others fear the kid gloves you wear because they have spikes on their tips. You are critical and rigid in the way you go about things; you leave no room for flow or play.

ADAPTIVE   You are impeccable in your methods of accomplishing things; at the same time, you are gentle and relaxed in your pace and tone. Others enjoy working with you because they know you can support them in achieving excellence—though not at the expense of a close feeling of bonding during the process.

EVOLVING   Your high standards for achievement are accompanied by a true appreciation for the joy of the present moment. You exude a sense of peacefulness in all you do because you are in love with each detail of each moment, regardless of flaws or mistakes. You are accountable for your choices, and you inspire others to choose wisely and with a great dose of self-acceptance.

Saturn in Libra

In this placement, Saturn's power can be diffused by indecision and shallow concerns about looks, image, and other avenues toward being pleasing to others rather than focusing on the real purpose at hand. Once the Saturn in Libra native figures out how to ground into the substance of a task, however, their approach becomes balanced, harmonizing, and elegant, rather than scattered.

PRIMITIVE Are you a little obsessed with your image? Perhaps you see yourself in too many mirrors. Is it hard to get under the patina of the project and dig into the substance? Is there just too much ambivalence to make a decision? It's hard to follow through when you have so many things to think about and so many people to please.

ADAPTIVE You possess extraordinary clarity and foresight in all endeavors. You see the balance of all things and head straight into the creation of a beautiful and substantial contribution. People remark on your style and depth, as well as the elegance with which you communicate your vision.

EVOLVING You are an avatar of emotional and social poise, emanating confidence based on true mastery and gentle competence. You are able to bring all sides to the table for the greater good. Your legacy is a seamless articulation of the beauty of doing things well and harmoniously.

Saturn in Scorpio

The unskillful Saturn in Scorpio native can be a sadist or a bully; when skillful, Saturn in Scorpio can build fiercely transformative movements, bringing people together in their deepest passions and persevering through obstacles of all kinds. This person can be known for their fearless confrontation of evil forces.

PRIMITIVE You'll put others on the medieval rack if they cross you. Your knuckles hurt from all the blows you have landed on yourself and others. You will prevail, no matter how low you have to go—and if necessary, you'll self-destruct to prove your point.

ADAPTIVE Your inner resolve matches your outer quiescence. You are able to stay focused and disciplined through distractions, detractors, and setbacks. People like to work beside you because it brings them intense satisfaction.

EVOLVING You transform metaphorical lead into gold. Negative energy becomes rocket fuel for immense social innovation and radical re-visioning. You touch into people's deepest core motivations. People realize the most noble and fruitful solutions in your presence.

Jemal, whose Saturn is in Scorpio, was raised by addicts. By the age of sixteen, he was hooked on heroin. He was also an accomplished musician, and while his heroin addiction did not interfere with his devotion to music, it did put his life in danger. By the time he was twenty-three, he had already come back from two overdoses, spending long periods in drug rehab programs.

By the time he was twenty-nine, he had relapsed again and spent time in prison. After his release at age thirty-one, he lived in a sober living home for two years, dedicating himself to teaching jazz music skills to residents. Jemal is currently working on a memoir based on his experience with turning darkness into dedicated creativity.

Saturn in Sagittarius

Sagittarius is ruled by Jupiter, Saturn's energetic opposite. Its expansive, freedom-loving energy is challenged by Saturn's hard boundaries and limitations. There can be a sense of being caught between optimistic hope and nihilistic pessimism. Skillfully expressed, this placement is a great setup for disciplined, clear transmission of knowledge; the pursuit of embodied learning and meaning; and expertise in applied principles and belief systems.

PRIMITIVE You're bombastic, righteous, exaggerated, inflated . . . but who's counting your blunders? You set off down a road and won't listen to any other options because your way is the right way. Others feel scolded and patronized by your high and mighty opinions.

ADAPTIVE You excel at setting a positive and open tone in any enterprise or venture. Others feel uplifted and buoyed by your sense of adventure, which is guided by a true north discipline and compass. Your warmth and enthusiasm are matched by your knowledge and accrued wisdom, and your decisions are trustworthy.

EVOLVING   You are a champion of all people's strengths and possibilities and the leader of leaps of progress. You are a visionary beside whom people love to work; you possess a contagion of optimism, coupled with groundbreaking strategies. Everyone's autonomy and opinion are prized and respected.

Saturn in Capricorn

Capricorn is ruled by Saturn, a planet that is most at home in this sign placement. It can mean following the rules, being concerned with reputation, and exhibiting steady discipline. The Saturn in Capricorn native has the fortitude to climb the mountain to its very top and isn't usually interested in breaking rules or pushing beyond the sure thing into riskier territory. Where unskillful, this same person can fall into a pattern of putting ambition above all else, getting stuck in overcaution, or becoming burnt out.

PRIMITIVE   Rules: rigid. Spine: erect. You are conservative and controlling. No one better make a false step unless it is you—and if it *is* you, you'll have no problem rationalizing it. You feel entirely justified in getting to the top in any way you can because you know full well that your brand is the superior one. The rules were not made for you; they're just for those other low-life folks.

ADAPTIVE   Backbone and fortitude are your social currency. People can rest on your enormous shoulders and enjoy the protections of your positive mood and countenance. You are reasonable and practical, and you can resonate with others' feelings in a way that is instructive.

EVOLVING   You have epic endurance and lasting values. You invite others into a stratosphere of excellence and grounded consciousness. People love to be part of your plans because you make things accessible, doable, and profoundly nourishing. You are the rock of responsibility that sits beside the pool of refreshing attitudes.

Saturn in Aquarius

Embracing fixed ideas—especially those that are either revolutionary or visionary—is part of Saturn in Aquarius's potential. The person with this placement is not afraid to break the rules; they don't need to conform to anyone else's way of doing things. Unskillful expression here can look like a rebel without a cause, squandering precious influence and energy and remaining disconnected from the beating heart of each individual's sovereignty.

PRIMITIVE   Fixed in perspective and unwilling to bend, you can be so blocked that nothing gets in. Adhering to tradition—or even to rebellion—your methods can be tyrannical; you feel entitled in this by your higher sight. Others can find your obstinacy and narrow-mindedness off-putting and harsh. Imperial and disconnected, you rule with coldness.

ADAPTIVE   Crystalline thinking guides you and others to attain spectacular heights. You exceed mortal expectations of distilled organization and planning. Your humanitarian heart enrolls others to offer their compassion and services for long-lasting improvements and policies.

EVOLVING   You represent the pinnacle of self-awareness and actualization to others. Flexible in perspective and steady in diligence, you activate the highest moral order in others. Your responsiveness to the cause is equal to your attention to the heart of each participant. You galvanize others through your emotional and social courage and humility.

Saturn in Pisces

Unskillful Saturn in Pisces may be revealed as challenges with planning, foresight, and follow-through, as well as a tendency to blame others when things don't go according to plan. More skillful expression strengthens the impact of Pisces's creative, expressive, empathic, intuitive nature, lending structure to one's dreams and one's bliss.

PRIMITIVE   You have been very taken by the image of the man on the cross—especially the part of the story where he is being nailed to it. Your narrative of victimization justifies your lack of follow-through on your ideas. Others have to pick up your emotional messes because you fail to recognize that your actions have consequences. Whining is your mode of agency.

ADAPTIVE   Within the deep bosom of altruism, you march forward, bringing others to the light. Your capacity for emotional resilience is laudatory, and others find you to be a balm of comfort during intense trials of suffering. Your willingness to work for the dream is unending, and you replenish yourself with constant spiritual practice.

EVOLVING You are a radiant version of *bodhisattva* consciousness. Your enlightened presence inspires others to raise their actions for the best of all. Others love to work alongside you; in doing so, they feel their hearts open and their creativity flourish. Wherever you go, you leave a sense of heaven on earth.

Josselin, whose Saturn is in Pisces, was raised by two progressive hippie activists. As a child, she thought it was normal to go to rallies once a month. She went to an unconventional middle and high school in which community service was a focal point of education, and she developed her own curriculum for an alternative high school in the town where she lived. Now a young adult, she hosts a once-yearly symposium on joining causes and leaders from the most avant-garde pioneering youth in the nation.

Practices for Saturn • • • • • • • • • •

Dive In

Pick one reasonable discipline to engage in each day—something that will support your character and growth. For example, meditate for ten minutes every morning and night or spend fifteen minutes per day organizing your space or your schedule.

Do this assignment every day at the same time for thirty days. Write a thank-you note to yourself each day for doing it. At the end of thirty days, offer yourself a small commendation prize for accomplishing this act.

To monumentally honor your Saturn—whatever its placement—repeat this thirty-day pledge for one year, with different disciplines for each month.

Reach Out

Pick someone in your life you can do a Saturn trade with. This person will coach you to learn and master something, and you will coach them to learn and master something in return. For example, you might have a friend teach you to cook Mexican food, while you teach the friend how to write articles.

Agree to work with each other until each of you has accomplished your goal. Do not allow setbacks to throw you off course. When either of you feels stopped by anything, simply regroup and head back to the finish line: this is Saturn's gift—not allowing obstacles to derail you.

Risk It

For one day, go and volunteer for a cause that has nothing to do with you or your self-interest. Give your whole day to this venture. Learn why it is crucial for others, as this will activate you in developing a sense of social responsibility that is altruistic instead of self-focused.

Reflect

Write a story or outline about how you learned about discipline: the good, the bad, and the ugly ways you were instructed. Parse out the best wisdom you have learned about being your word and doing the work. Notice which methods or advice have been unhelpful.

Then, write a contract with yourself about recommitting to disciplinary methods that actually bring the best out of you.

Talking Circle Questions

Gather with one or more people who have read this chapter. Using a talking piece everyone has agreed on (see note to "Talking Circle Questions" in chapter 2), have each person answer the following questions, one at a time. Make sure there is no cross-talk or side-talk; this is a time for completely undistracted, uninterrupted sharing. Before beginning, agree to keep what is said in the circle confidential, to listen deeply, to speak without rehearsing, and to be aware of time so that all have a chance to answer each question in the time available.

1. Talk about how your upbringing did—or did not—prepare you for the true responsibilities of adulthood.

2. How do you approach your responsibilities today? What is your attitude toward work?

3. How have you overcome your worst adversities? Who or what helped you?

4. Who have been your role models in their work ethic? Why?

5. If you were to leave behind only one legacy, what would it be?

6. Name one thing you wish you would have followed through on and what difference it would have made.

7. Talk about one thing you need support to follow through on. What difference will it make to you and others when you do follow through on it?

[T]he world sometimes feels like the
waiting room of the emergency ward. . . .
We who are more or less OK for now
need to take the tenderest possible care
of the more wounded people in
the waiting room, until the healer comes.

ANNE LAMOTT

The great illusion of leadership
is to think that man can be led
out of the desert by someone
who has never been there.

HENRI J.M. NOUWEN

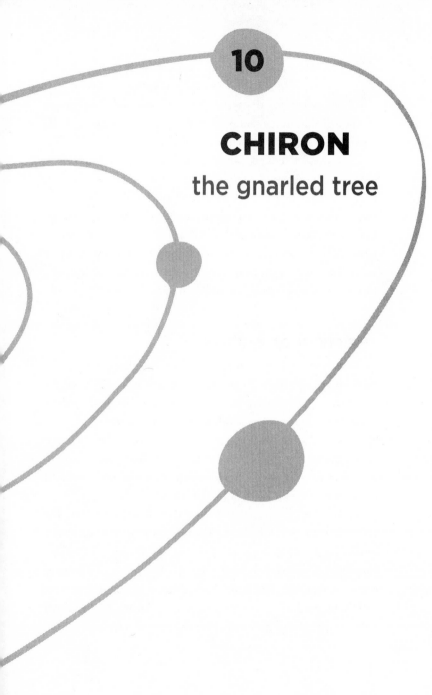

CHIRON

the gnarled tree

Chiron is an orbiting comet that is regarded as a "minor planet" in modern psychological astrology. It represents the archetype of the wounded healer—a symbol of the fundamental truth that a person who has been wounded is best able to help others heal.

In a broader sense, Chiron reminds us that we must examine our own personal wounds if we are to be sensitive to the needs of others. While some of us have wounds that might seem more severe and damaging than those life has inflicted upon others, the presence of Chiron in every birth chart reminds us that to live is to be wounded—somehow, in some way—and that we all have healing to do. We also all have the capacity to bring healing to others in need.

THE MYTH OF CHIRON

In Greek mythology, Chiron was one of the Centaurs—a race of part-human, part-horse creatures who lived in the mountains. Chiron was known for his wisdom and medical knowledge. He was the product of a union between the god Kronus and a nymph named Philyra, who was so uninterested in mating with Kronus that she turned herself into a mare in an effort to turn him off. He turned himself into a stallion, satisfied himself, and left her in the dust.

Philyra gave birth to Chiron and then abandoned him. The myth then has him adopted by the Greek sun god, Apollo, who taught Chiron so much that he became a well-respected teacher himself. Chiron was then accidentally wounded in one knee with an arrow that had been dipped in the blood of a monster called the Hydra—a treatment known to create a wound that will never heal and that will cause enormous pain.

Because he was immortal, Chiron was stuck with a painful wound that would not heal for all eternity. Only when he switched places with Prometheus—who had been chained to a rock for stealing fire from Olympia and giving it over to mortals and who was condemned to have an eagle eat a piece of his liver every day only to heal and face another day of the same—was Chiron able to give up his immortal status. His eventual death released him from his suffering. Since then, he has appeared in the night sky as the constellation Centaurus.

THE GNARLED TREE

A gnarled tree stands tall, making no apologies for its unique form—wounds and all. When we fully embrace our wounds and our specific emotional histories, we come to a healing place, inside and out. As we accept the reality of what is and what has been, others can find refuge in our shade and find grace within themselves.

Chiron as the gnarled tree reminds us of our wholeness, including our emotional or physical wounds or deformities.

CHIRON IN THE SIGNS

The sign placement of Chiron in our birth chart can give us valuable insight into a place in ourselves where we hold deep woundedness and where the healing of that wound can make us uniquely able to serve others' healing.

Chiron in Aries

It's widely accepted that hurt people hurt people, and the impulsive, immature, willful, selfish side of Aries can make unhealed hurt a weapon that can do a lot of damage. More skillful expression that comes with self-healing makes the Chiron in Aries native an energized bringer of help who can lift others with strength and forceful grace.

PRIMITIVE From an early age, you've felt rejected and spurned. You resort to bullying tactics to get your way. Stubbornly, you cling to this strategy—even as, time and time again, it gets you in trouble. You see fault in others when this happens, which enables you to continue your reign of terror.

ADAPTIVE Heroic and humble, you stride forward to assist others in finding their strengths. You realize the importance of diplomacy and deep listening in all your endeavors. People depend on you for the resilient, stable strength that comes from maturity.

EVOLVING You are an exemplar of social and emotional skill; you are exceptionally considerate of others' needs as you pioneer into uncharted territories of reformation. Everyone enjoys the warm fire of confidence you evoke in them.

Throughout his childhood, Dave—a Chiron in Aries—suffered from chronic migraines. When he was sixteen, he was involved in a car accident where he sustained a serious head injury. Many years following were spent frequenting rehabilitation centers and doctors' offices. Dave was angry about his situation and often took it out on others.

After a few years of failed relationships and dead-end attempts to find his right livelihood, he realized he had a real talent with understanding head injuries. He studied to become an osteopath. Now, his full-time work is helping people with brain injuries—his very wound became his healing profession.

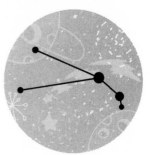

Chiron in Taurus

The earthy influence of Taurus suggests both wounding and healing around physical safety or the safety of one's surroundings, which may include home, community, or the entire planet. This placement can impact safety and security of one's own body, of the bodies of other people, of objects and possessions, or of the Earth itself.

PRIMITIVE You often feel ugly or unworthy, weighed down by a burden of shame. A belief that you are unable to cherish others or feel loved yourself eats away at you. You often feel haunted by a sense of being betrayed by your body in some critical way.

ADAPTIVE Seeing beauty in the worn and tattered, you infuse tossed-away people and possessions with new life. You can see through surfaces to the gorgeous layers underneath, and you make a point of celebrating them.

EVOLVING By realizing the potentials of recyclables and trash, you create useful community art and added value. You transform people's notions of aesthetics to include the scars and blemishes inflicted by a fully lived life.

Chiron in Gemini

Gemini's wounding and healing usually have to do with language, communication, and ideas. Unskillful Chiron in Gemini can recall William Faulkner's "sound and fury, signifying nothing." As skill is built, the power of words and thought are increasingly applied to improving one's own life and the lives of others. Chiron in Gemini can also indicate learning differences that can either hold people back or give them perspectives that other people can't access.

PRIMITIVE   Word salad is your specialty; so is gossip that aims to maim. Feeling deeply insecure about your intelligence causes you to make fun of others. You use your mouth as a spigot of maliciousness against yourself and others.

ADAPTIVE   You are acutely sensitive and skillful at promoting positive dialogue. People feel safe discussing vulnerable subjects and concerns with you because you handle their confidences with supreme care.

EVOLVING   Whether in public speaking or writing, you use your immense experience and compassion to educate people about oppression. You are devoted to uncovering lies and hidden agendas. You bring fresh air to earnest stories and perspectives.

Chiron in Cancer

Healing of woundedness around emotions, abandonment, mothering or being mothered, and the feminine are supported through a skillful living out of Chiron in Cancer. As those with this sign work through their abandonment wounds, they are able to help others who have felt cast out by their important caregivers.

PRIMITIVE A feeling of being rejected and abandoned by the feminine colors your view. You act as if the world owes you something. People constantly disappoint you when they can't predict your needs. You are deeply cynical about adulthood and refuse to grow up.

ADAPTIVE You have notably cultivated your nurturing abilities and created a solid balance between emotions and logic. You help others feel safe and loved and can skillfully quell others' intemperate drives.

EVOLVING Extraordinarily composed and compassionate people are drawn to your emotional equanimity. You lead others to protect the fragile, and you serve from a selfless place. You feel constantly renewed by the well of divine energy running through you.

Sylvia's Chiron is in the sign of Cancer. She lost her mother at the age of eight. Her father, inconsolable and bereft, became a crack addict. Throughout three years spent homeless and in shelters, Sylvia endured unspeakable suffering—yet she still managed to stay caught up in school.

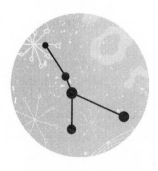

In junior high, Sylvia's math teacher identified her as someone with incredible aptitude. This teacher helped her get into a private boarding school specializing in science and math. Sylvia graduated from Yale with her PhD and became a well-respected professor of mathematics. Her classes are favorites with students because of the theatrical bent she brings to even the most mundane of lessons.

Chiron in Leo

When expressed through Leo, Chiron can bring pointless drama and an unending craving for approval and acknowledgment. Or it can be an expansive, powerful force that heals through bigness of heart, creativity, and pure radiant love. Chiron in Leo can also indicate a theft of childhood, in which one tries constantly to either regain or heal the hurts of the inner child.

PRIMITIVE Torn apart by lost love, you repeat self-defeating patterns of lack over and over again. Your failure to see the true needs and motivations of others hurls you into unhealthy relationships. Looking too much for mirroring costs you your self-respect.

ADAPTIVE You have an acute eye for people who are in need of tender loving care. You give this attention in a clean way, without attachment. People feel healed by your openhearted welcoming of all their strengths and frailties.

EVOLVING Your magnanimous nature spills gloriously onto everyone you meet. Your bold laughter creates gaiety wherever you go. You remind people how to fully enjoy the story as it unfolds, including the bumpy ride they may have to endure along the way.

Chiron in Virgo

The sign of Virgo already brings a focus on joining body, mind, and spirit in healthy ways—an important foundation for any kind of healing. This placement can push healing back behind barriers of self-criticism and sometimes illness. It can mean seeing everything through a negative lens: focusing on all that is wrong and staying stuck in patterns of creating and re-creating the same problems. Skillful Chiron in Virgo mines this sign's detail orientation and patience, supporting presence and comfort with process over product in healing one's self and others.

PRIMITIVE   Prone to judgmental and pessimistic thinking, you get locked into negative states for long periods. Insufferable criticism and a sense of personal insufficiency underlie your approach with others. You keep shooting yourself in the foot.

ADAPTIVE   You excel at making others feel good about learning from mistakes. Your tactics and strategies involve lots of room for trial and error. There is no end to your patience with the process and with helping others stay on task.

EVOLVING   Impeccably accepting of others, you lead the way in finding the gold in any apparent flaw. You heal people with your precise understanding of their self-doubt and guide them toward their greatest capabilities. You take great joy in mind-body-spirit health because you understand that holistic well-being is foundational for a life of clarity.

Chiron in Libra

Balance and beauty are Libra's most prominent energies. When linked with the wounded healer archetype, Libra can keep one stuck in a focus on appearances and the outside impression of beauty, creating and re-creating wounds around a feeling of never being *enough*. Skillful expression means applying Libra's innate harmoniousness to people and circumstances outside one's self to promote healing at both the individual and the collective level.

PRIMITIVE Being caught in a web of self-deception and image obsession makes it hard to feel at home in yourself. Others are repelled by the polite face you wear plastered over what's really going on; they do not trust your motives. Someone wants you to show up somewhere for them? You might say yes—until something better comes along. As a result, people feel like pawns in your social life.

ADAPTIVE Aware of beauty in the smallest of gestures and inside the purity of noble character, you express a genuine appreciation of real gifts. Inspired by fairness and harmony, you extol opportunities for others to find true balance in relationships.

EVOLVING Divine curiosity leads you to great adventures of innovation and companionship. Others find your enlightened approach to creating art from any medium awe-evoking. Your essential beauty transcends all limitations of size, age, gender, and other surface concerns.

Maggie, whose Chiron is in Libra, grew up in Argentina in the 1950s—a period of revolution, financial instability, censorship, and the torture and killing of those who opposed the regime then in power. She endured constant fear and witnessed bombings and massacres. The trauma she experienced hardened her; she became hyper-focused on cultivating her exterior beauty and climbing the social ladder. She lived a shallow life and did not delve into parts of herself that were calling out for healing.

Things turned around for her when, as a young adult, she left her home country to study mediation in the United States. This course of study required her to investigate her own past in some depth and to do the work of healing her own traumas so that she could be exquisitely present for others working through conflict.

Once she had established superlative skill as a mediator, she chose to return to Argentina in this capacity to support her home country in healing.

Chiron in Scorpio

Trauma and wounding are important issues in this placement, especially around topics of sexuality and death. A person with Chiron in Scorpio may find their way through healing their own abuse; the alternative is more exposure to darkness. Building skill here means using the passion and emotional depths of Scorpio to heal the self and to help others meaningfully heal trauma.

PRIMITIVE You live from past hurts, compulsively stinging yourself and others. Your penchant for meanness controls you. Your criminal and destructive tendencies don't stop you from blaming others for your actions. At the same time, you cannot understand why other people avoid you.

ADAPTIVE You know just how to turn unskillful emotions into learning opportunities. Others come to you to face dark nights of the soul with courage. You are fully accountable for the past and recognize how to unlock unconscious patterns in yourself and others.

EVOLVING You have transcended the fear of dying; you therefore live a daring and expressive life dedicated to transforming pain into spiritual awakening. Others find their own resolute authenticity in your presence and glow from the burning embers of your aliveness.

Chiron in Sagittarius

With Chiron in Sagittarius, wounding may come in some way through a call to adventure or in being drawn to higher learning that then turns out to be hollow or even false. Skillful healing through this placement means fanning the flames of one's natural bent toward joy and optimism, as well as through steadfast self-care around physical and mental well-being and disciplined study. This path enables one to be more exemplary in caring for others.

PRIMITIVE You have been so disillusioned by false ideologies that you find life meaningless. Depressed by the seeming endless cruelty and drudgery of life, you have trouble rebounding from continual disappointments. You are obsessed with news programs that confirm your worst fear—that humans are hopelessly doomed.

ADAPTIVE   You work hard at honing perspectives that find the best in everything. Your emotional resilience is based on a thorough understanding of wisdom traditions. Others find your natural joy a relief to be around—a break from the seductive cultural background noise of anger, fear, and frustration.

EVOLVING   Your diligent practical study of the relevance and impact of optimism has given you a direct experience of altering your own neural pathways for the better. Others come to you to learn to reset their minds and move from post-traumatic stress to post-traumatic growth. You are known far and wide as a model of mind-body wisdom.

Chiron in Capricorn

Wounded by the structures in which one has felt forced to try to fit in, belong, and do the right thing, the Chiron in Capricorn native may express unskillfully by doubling down on their attachment to shreds and shards of old belief systems and outworn habits. Skillful Chiron in Capricorn lets go of the content of what has harmed them to focus on applying their prodigious discipline and foresight to building new systems that work for everyone.

PRIMITIVE   Ruined by the failure of patriarchal culture to provide stability and discipline, you continuously self-sabotage. You cannot fathom why the world refuses to bend to your will. Others feel alternately sorry for you and scared of your contemptuous anger.

ADAPTIVE   Your integrity underlies everything you say and do. You have learned the right use of power, and you feel at home with enormous responsibilities. As an advocate for healing toxic masculinity, you reflect a healthy relationship with assertion and boundaries.

EVOLVING You are known for your humble competency. Others rely on you for clear guidance in developing their aptitudes. You exude hard-won confidence by treating failures as minor speed bumps on the way to learning. Others remark on your composure and your cultural sensitivity.

Jimmy has Chiron in Capricorn. He grew up in a very poor immigrant family—so poor that, on many occasions, they went without food. Still, his parents fought for him to get ahead, and he did all he needed to do to get his education. The trials he faced sometimes led him to sabotage himself: he became attached to things being a certain way and could not adjust his expectations, eventually ending up in trouble for venting his frustration in unskillful ways.

He persevered with the support of his family and others who knew his loyal, steadfast heart and his willingness and capableness in the face of enormous amounts of responsibility. He ended up as an executive at a major international bank, where he was able to make full use of his bilingual skills and his lived experience of adversity.

Chiron in Aquarius

Allowing one's wounds to create separateness from others and to drive one into a state of emotional numbness or remove would be an unskillful expression of this placement. Being willing to be both unique in one's woundedness and accepting of every kind of wound—recognizing how healing is a community endeavor—would be the way to a more skillful expression of Chiron in Aquarius.

PRIMITIVE Your alienation from others creates a hardened defensiveness—an android-like, superior posturing. You hide out in thinking that others just don't understand a unique genius like you. Your cold, utilitarian approach to relationship confirms your worst fear—that you will always be emotionally isolated.

ADAPTIVE You are an ambassador for the freaks and the geeks because you deeply understand being misunderstood. You proudly own your quirk factor and inspire others to be less inhibited. Your overall sense of everyone fitting in somewhere is a safe haven for all who know you.

EVOLVING Your embrace of the humanity in all people encourages a true openness in others. You see beyond party and identity lines to a whole, connected community. Your work in social empathy building creates pathways of understanding for everyone.

Chiron in Pisces

This placement can bring difficulty in releasing victim thinking or managing the deep waters of the emotions that surround and flow from our wounds. Building greater skill here means finding ways to bring compassion outward to the world: to bathe others in a warm sea of care, to accept what is and to support others in doing the same, and to be the safe harbor they have needed to face the world's inevitable challenges.

PRIMITIVE   Feeling somehow cursed by the gods, you cast yourself as a hopeless victim of circumstance. Others try to rescue you, only to feel your wrath later as their efforts ultimately fail. Your life is a banquet of excuses and rationalization for not living the dream and for being left out of the bliss.

ADAPTIVE   You exhibit preternatural grace in all situations. Your profound understanding of life's mysteries enables you to see beyond ego-oriented suffering. Others come to you to be forgiven for their entrenched unhappiness and to find solace in your grand heart.

EVOLVING   You are a *bodhisattva* of human compassion. Your kindness is effusive and soft, providing a giant landing pad for others' suffering. You have a devoted spiritual practice that allows you to ride towering waves of sadness and joy with gratitude. You see life as an unending education in acceptance.

Practices for Chiron • • • • • • • • • •

Dive In

Write about your earliest experiences of being wounded in the way your Chiron description relates; notice key decision points about yourself or others. Write about how you might upgrade them in the present to reflect your placement's most positive possibilities.

Reach Out

Find someone in your life who currently feels hurt by some type of emotional poison arrow. Tell them you would like to simply listen to them for an hour and be with them in their pain, without solving anything.

This will be a miracle.

Risk It

Write a song or poem about your Chiron struggle and sing or read it to at least one person.

Reflect

Think of a time when you had your greatest healing in terms of your Chiron wound. Write five components to that healing. Re-create those conditions as best you can.

Talking Circle Questions

Gather with one or more people who have read this chapter. Using a talking piece everyone has agreed on (see note to "Talking Circle Questions" in chapter 2), have each person answer the following questions, one at a time. Make sure there is no cross-talk or side-talk; this is a time for completely undistracted, uninterrupted sharing. Before beginning, agree to keep what is said in the circle confidential, to listen deeply, to speak without rehearsing, and to be aware of time so that all have a chance to answer each question in the time available.

1. Name a time when you felt the worst of your wounded nature.

2. Name a time when you experienced a profound healing.

3. Talk about a time when you helped heal someone. How did you do this?

4. What do you admire most in a healer?

5. Name a time when a healer was actually hurtful to you and explain why.

6. What conditions most bring out your healing capacities?

7. Tell each person in the group one thing you find healing about them.

Those who make peaceful revolution impossible will make violent revolution inevitable.

JOHN F. KENNEDY

Like art, revolutions come from combining what exists into what has never existed before.

GLORIA STEINEM

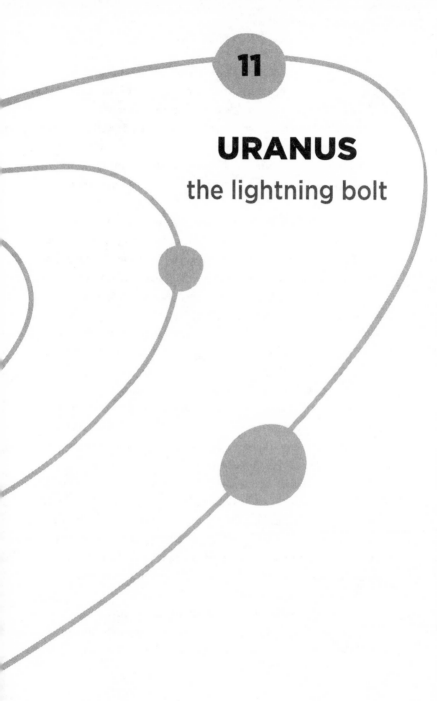

11

URANUS
the lightning bolt

Uranus represents the archetype of sudden change, lightning transformations, bursts of insight, and "a-ha moments." It represents the spirit of revolution, reinvention, and overturning of the status quo, as well as of our capacity for innovation, change, and collective freedom.

With the outer planets—Uranus, Neptune, and Pluto—the personal and the transpersonal merge. Within generations, people born in a range of years all share the same sign placements for these three planets. All the people born between October 1968 and September 1975, for example, share the placement of Uranus in Libra; those born between June 1934 and May 1942 share the placement of Uranus in Taurus. It follows that in each period of seven or eight years, a group of individuals will express the same revolutionary tendencies, reflective of the sign placement of that planet during that era.

This chapter includes date ranges for Uranus placements in the signs. As you look at Uranus in your own birth chart and consider how it can be expressed in ways that are Primitive, Adaptive, or Evolving, recognize that your peers within that same range have this same placement and are likely to express the same elements you are or have been expressing. Realize that world events during this same period in history will also reflect that sign placement.

Rather than describing each placement in terms of how *you* might express it individually, I'll take a broader perspective that appreciates the collective nature of the outer planets' expression. In place of the general description of the individual's traits and growing edges for each placement, I will list a few world events or trends from that period.

Those born while Uranus is in the signs listed here will express on an individual level the same potentials and possibilities described in their sections, as will all others who were born during that same time frame. As the collective moves its Uranus expression from Primitive to Adaptive to Evolving, so too can the people who mirror it in their own birth charts.

If you were born in a year listed at the start or finish of the time span under one sign and your birth chart shows you in another, you may have come into the world in the months before or after Uranus arrived in or left that sign.

THE MYTH OF URANUS

Uranus is a god from Greek mythology, born from primeval Chaos, along with the mountains and the oceans. The union of Gaia (Earth) and Uranus produced several races, including the Titans and the Cyclopes. Uranus didn't much like the offspring they'd created, so he hid them away inside Gaia. A Titan named Kronos decided to help Gaia liberate them by castrating Uranus and throwing his genitals into the ocean. The blood that flowed from this wound fell onto the earth, giving rise to additional races of creatures, including the Furies and the Giants. Severed from his body, Uranus's genitals floated on the sea and produced a white foam from which rose the goddess Aphrodite.

THE LIGHTNING BOLT

Uranus hosts a non-binary and all-inclusive energy of social and cultural awakening. It is associated with liberation periods and dramatic movements, where a cultural or historical pendulum swing changes direction and oppressed or marginalized people rise up. The metaphor of lightning striking fits this archetype in both positive (the proverbial "a-ha moment") and negative ways. Its skillful implications are the lightning bolt of intuition, the "eureka!" breakthrough;

its unskillful side—the immediate, electrocuting destruction that comes with a bolt of lightning striking a person or structure—reflects its less skillful expression.

URANUS IN THE SIGNS

The sign placement of Uranus in your birth chart gives insight into the ways in which revolutionary, surprising breakthroughs and intuitive change either come from you or are likely to happen to you. You share these characteristics with others who were born around the same time you were born. The "you" of the Primitive, Adaptive, and Evolving descriptions that follow reflects both the individual "you" *and* the collective of folks who share this placement with you; it also reflects the times in which you have lived.

When you block the expression of Uranus in your life, the universe has a way of making Uranian inventions anyhow: they happen *to* you instead of coming from you.

Uranus in Aries

1927-1934 AND 2010-2018

In Aries, Uranus's expressions can come through outright rebellion and aggressive struggles against the status quo or through selfless heroism and fearless action taken on behalf of those in need and in the name of social progress.

In the time frame of 1927–1934, Wall Street crashed cataclysmically, and the Great Depression set in. In early 1930s' Germany, Adolf Hitler and the Nazi Party came to power. In 1927, penicillin was discovered, and Charles Lindbergh made his historic trans-Atlantic flight.

In 2010, financial markets were tailspinning once again in the context of the global financial crisis that gained steam in the late 2000s. US military involvement ramped up in the Middle East and Central America, and whistle-blower individuals and organizations like Edward Snowden and WikiLeaks published classified information and revealed global surveillance strategies of the National Security Agency.

PRIMITIVE   You unleash warlike energy to whip up rebellion and antiestablishment sentiments, creating havoc through impulsive, egoic actions. You don't care about the cost to human lives or feelings. You uplift the mighty few at the expense of the rest.

ADAPTIVE   You use courage and conviction to move toward a society that takes care of the least privileged and the most needy. You take on the hard task of breaking through self-interest on behalf of the community at large.

EVOLVING   You practice true, egoless heroism, using strengths and resources for social progress tied to empathy and the well-being of every creature and human—and of the Earth itself.

Uranus in Taurus

1934–1941 AND 2018–2025

Citizen Kane—named by many as the best movie ever made—was released in 1941; its main character, who sets out to do good and be of service with the means at his disposal but ends up ruthlessly pursuing power and wealth, is an excellent illustration of the potential and pitfalls of Uranus in Taurus. During that time, World War II was ramping up, as Germany and the Soviet Union invaded several countries apiece in a set of highly destructive and vastly scaled resource grabs.

At this writing in 2019, the neoliberal, materialistic free-for-all seems to be coming to a point of unsustainability. During the remaining years of this placement, we are poised to move into a more skillful version of Uranus in Taurus: a green revolution where greater socioeconomic equality is realized.

PRIMITIVE You tend toward wild and eccentric use of materials, money, and land, feeling entitled to create a niche of superior wealth. You are distanced and detached from the consequences of reckless spending and lack of planning.

ADAPTIVE You generate inventive and creative ways to heal the planet. Your practicality and out-of-the-box thinking combine to bring true solutions to entrenched problems.

EVOLVING You develop extraordinary mind-sets about collective ways to balance uneven distribution of resources, seeing materialism as a means to the end of solving the problems of world poverty, starvation, and climate change.

Uranus in Gemini

1941–1948

During this time, the world saw the Manhattan Project; the bombing of Hiroshima and Nagasaki; and the development of radar, jet aircraft, commercial TV, microwaves, Velcro, the very first computer, and quantum physics. This period heralded a huge number of important scientific discoveries, connections, and ideas that altered humanity forever.

In 1943, Ayn Rand's famous novel *The Fountainhead* was published; in 1944, French playwright Jean-Paul Sartre's *No Exit* was first produced. These works reflect Gemini qualities: Rand's novel celebrates individualistic, self-focused, abstract thinking over a focus on the good of the collective, and Sartre's play about three damned people driving one another crazy with words, ideas, and more words in a tastefully appointed room comes to a climax with its most famous line, "Hell is other people."

PRIMITIVE Caught in dispersive and chaotic energy, your loose words cause havoc and anxiety. There is such a lack of substance and character that communications are dangerous—sometimes ruinous.

ADAPTIVE Electric and brilliant ideas abound; your mind is a clear bell of foresight and insight. People rally around your forward-thinking methods and policies.

EVOLVING Sparks of illumination and enlightenment encourage the masses to be more conscious and aware. Communications travel quickly and effectively, getting to the heart of the matter and liberating people from false narratives of fear.

Uranus in Cancer

1948–1955

When Uranus was last in the sign of Cancer, between 1948 and 1955, the world saw conflict and social change driven by emotionality, by obsolete ways of viewing others, and by unrealistic ideals about safety. Apartheid laws passed in South Africa to enforce racial segregation and discrimination ramped up significantly. The Korean War began in 1950; eventually, twenty-one countries belonging to the United Nations took part in the war effort against North Korean forces, which were supported by China and the Soviet Union.

From 1950–1955, Joseph McCarthy spearheaded the famous hearings designed to ferret out Communists "hiding" in plain sight in the United States. The word *McCarthyism* is still used to describe the public defamation of someone with wild allegations fueled by unskillful emotions or by fear for the safety of one's self or one's people.

PRIMITIVE   Clinging to old and outworn ideas of emotional patterns and social roles, you are infantilized instead of being called to greater maturity. The tantrums of a few get folks stirred up and engaged in fake notions of security.

ADAPTIVE   You are freed from confining notions of gender and gender roles, and the world of mutuality begins to grow. Realizing that empathy is the start of social progress helps you align with goals for healthy homes and families.

EVOLVING   Combining great wisdom from the ages with a new frontier of possibility, you seek a common universal language of feeling and connection. Knowing that each person desires a place of belonging in the world, you work to create a planet that hosts everyone as beloved.

Sally, born during a Uranus in Cancer period, was raised in a Midwestern conservative home. Her family expected her to marry at an early age and to devote her life to being a dutiful wife and mother. Although she followed that prescription to a "T" throughout her twenties and most of her thirties—marrying a suitable man and having the prototypical "fulfilling" life of wife and mother—things changed dramatically in her thirty-ninth year. With a sudden, lightning-like shift, Sally unexpectedly fell in love with a woman and realized it was her dream to pursue a writing career. Subsequently, her notions of home, family, and career were completely rearranged. Sally went on to live a vibrant life in her partnership and became a prolific and well-respected writer.

Uranus in Leo

1955–1961

When Uranus was last in Leo, the modern solar cell was invented—definitely a skillful expression of this sunny placement (Leo is ruled by the Sun). Pop music was born with the rise to fame of Elvis Presley, Chuck Berry, the Platters, the Drifters, and other artists who appealed most strongly to the teen market. This was also considered the "golden age of television." As television became a major part of modern life, however, so too did the comparison obsession and the "keeping up with the Joneses" mind-set that this medium has continued to augment and accelerate from that time forward.

Other surges in the creative zeitgeist, which are also skillful expressions of Uranus in Leo, include the evolution of abstract impressionism (including the work of painters like Jackson Pollock) and other visual artists who drew from pop culture images to build their work.

PRIMITIVE Self-obsessed and narcissistically motivated, you cannot get enough self-help to satisfy your need. Imposter gurus and charlatan growth teachers lead people into more emptiness through navel gazing.

ADAPTIVE   Listening to each person's authentic story allows you to collaborate on big ideas related to the creation of a world community. Arts and entertainment become a way for you to nourish social causes and bring people of all ages and demographics together.

EVOLVING   Self-realization is an avenue toward total self-lessness, where the ego is transcended in favor of promoting the well-being of others. Your creativity is a fountain of original and liberating energy, used to free the collective from past shackles of self-consciousness and a lack of self-acceptance.

Uranus in Virgo

1961–1968

When Uranus was last in Virgo, much of the Western world was embroiled in the "swinging sixties"—a revolutionary time in terms of social mores and sexuality. Ideas about schooling changed a lot during this time as well, and in most Western nations, politics swung dramatically leftward. An economic boom, the Vietnam War, the draft (and the huge rise in college attendance that happened at the same time), the Cuban missile crisis, the assassination of John F. Kennedy, Martin Luther King Jr.'s "I Have a Dream" speech—all these circumstances reflect the tension between the Uranian inevitability of revolution and innovation and the staid, organized, detail-oriented, and possibly fearful or stubborn energy of Virgo.

PRIMITIVE   Nervously, anxiously, you worry about every possible negative scenario, while failing to focus on what is going well and the ways in which coping and caring can be strengthened. Judgment and pettiness are the predominant defenses of this placement.

ADAPTIVE The integration of mind, body, feeling, and spirit becomes paramount, as does recognizing the power of thoughts in terms of creating well-being and mental health. Precision and impeccability are raised to a higher art form; you inspire others to work steadily on their attitudes and habits.

EVOLVING The mastery of skillful speech and refined actions is highlighted here. A Zen-like clarity surfaces in the ways you communicate and get things done, elevating the details while bringing appreciation of the overall flow of life.

Uranus in Libra
1968–1974

Women's liberation, tension between the forces of capitalist and communist regimes, and an ongoing rise in socially progressive values—all were hallmarks of 1968–1974, which is the last time Uranus occupied the sign of Libra. Humanity began to deeply question and investigate unequal social structures and to look at the pattern of the more powerful colonizing the less powerful. The Stonewall uprising—a series of rebellious demonstrations by the LGBT community against police raids in Greenwich Village—occurred in 1969, a brutal and essential wakeup call now considered to be the true beginning of the fight for LGBT rights in the United States.

In Libra, Uranus reminds us that none of us are free until all of us are free.

If that's not Libra enough for you, also consider that the very first face-lifts were attempted during this time!

PRIMITIVE Defined social norms of beauty and relationship become a fanatical drive. You are compelled to disrupt harmony for the sake of a shock. Themes of ugliness and heartbreak are constantly reiterated.

ADAPTIVE Highlighting the unconventional in beauty and relationships provides breakthroughs from oppressive gender norms. New paradigms of relationship offer relief from unconscious and unequal norms of all kinds.

EVOLVING Civil rights are prized, and the liberation of marginalized sectors is promised. You work across all special interests to find common ground where all can be welcomed and honored in their particular and shared concerns.

Uranus in Scorpio
1974–1981

In Scorpio, Uranus's elements of surprise take on potentially terrifying dimensions, embroiling humanity in the most intense of concerns around death, transformation, and sexuality. Between 1974 and 1981, the Khmer Rouge took power in Cambodia, torturing and massacring two million people (in particular, educated people, though many others were also targeted) in an obviously misguided attempt to establish a utopian Marxist society. In 1978, cult leader Jim Jones was responsible for leading 918 of his followers to suicide at the Peoples Temple compound in Guyana. US authorities were investigating Jones for human rights abuses against his followers; he decided for all of them that they should all die in protest rather than allowing him to face the consequences of his actions. (What many people don't know about Jim Jones is that he did a great deal of humanitarian work and fought for racial and socioeconomic justice—an illustration of the scope of the light and dark of Uranus in Scorpio.)

This period also saw the Iranian revolution and Iran hostage crisis; the decolonization of Africa, which led to famine and civil war; and the overthrow of the democratically elected Socialist government of Chile (an effort the United States supported, despite widespread torture and execution of those who opposed or seemed to oppose this change).

Meanwhile, the first-ever mainstream hard-core porn film, *Behind the Green Door*, was released in theaters across the United States. The sexual revolution continued to flourish, and homosexuality became more accepted in some parts of the world. Hard rock and punk rock were popular, and hip-hop began to emerge. The light and the dark, the mysterious and the terrifying, the transformational and the tormented all showed up at both grand and small scales during this Uranus in Scorpio period.

PRIMITIVE This placement brings a delving into dark and shadowy sides of sex and power, where abuse and harms are revealed. It can be a secret trap door of destructive and dangerous behaviors, rationalized by amoral perspectives.

ADAPTIVE Revolutionary attitudes take sex and power out of the shadows to be dealt with in open, constructive dialogue. Those who have been forced to closet themselves due to long-held prejudices can emerge again and be redeemed. There is a new frontier of experimentation around the occult and a more active imagination around issues of death and dying.

EVOLVING Shared power becomes more possible as the breakdown of historic *-isms* is fueled by the recognition that all people are worthy and valuable. Primary attention is paid to the transformative energies of true intimacy and intentional healing modalities based on the power of psychic and clairsentient abilities.

Chad, born during a Uranus in Scorpio period, was brought up in a bohemian artist family, where his parents actively fostered all his creative talents. Although his family had a joyful and abundant sense of possibility, Chad began to feel inexorably drawn to the dark side of creativity. He felt a deep fascination with murder mysteries, and by the time he was twenty-one, he had decided to become a murder mystery novelist. Chad spends his spare time watching the Surgery Channel, which fulfills his intense day-to-day need for transformational drama.

Uranus in Sagittarius

1981–1988

After the dark times of Uranus in Scorpio, the passage of Uranus into Sagittarius brought in fiery, forward-moving, connecting, positive energy and knowledge that felt much needed. In 1985, the world came together around the sixteen-hour Live Aid concert, with billions watching and contributing, raising just under two million dollars to help relieve the famine in Ethiopia. Millions more dollars were raised through the sale of a single, "Do They Know It's Christmas?" which was recorded for the event by a huge group of the era's most famous musicians.

The impact of human activity on climate change was first recognized during this time. The first multinational corporations were born. The global Internet formed, and people across the Third World joined the rest of the world in obtaining televisions—two shifts that began to link humanity like never before.

PRIMITIVE Beliefs are peddled like merchandise as a solution to all inadequacies. Snake charmers emerge everywhere, cajoling folks to trade their dignity for the latest cult idea or fad. Discernment is lost to blind faith.

ADAPTIVE Wisdom religions and practices make a comeback as people yearn for rituals of meaning. You begin to understand that knowledge truly is power, so you prioritize education and learning from other cultures. Happiness and joy are popular again; methods to achieve these conditions take on more status.

EVOLVING Inventiveness and exploration allow people all over the globe to imagine a world without walls or divisions. Old, outworn ideas of separation crumble in favor of noble truths of interdependency. Folks gather together to raise the roof with revelry, raves, concerts, and other celebrations that help them remember their colorful tribal nature.

Uranus in Capricorn
1904–1912 AND 1988–1995

The building of the Panama Canal and the publication of Upton Sinclair's novel *The Jungle*—a book that sought to reveal the ways in which immigrants were being exploited and subjected to extremely punishing work conditions and the corrupt ways in which powerful entities were profiting from their suffering—fell within this first time span. Systems that disregard some people's humanity in favor of enriching a select few were rapidly becoming entrenched, demonstrating how the clear thinking and future planning characteristic of this sign placement can be used to foment either good or evil on a world scale.

Between 1988 and 1995, the world saw continued growth of neoliberal economics. The North American Free Trade Agreement was passed, creating a free trade zone for Canada, Mexico, and the United States. While power and wealth were being directed and consolidated into the hands of a powerful few and as economic and political power shifted and solidified in various ways that reinforced this pattern, the world's attention was diverted by a shiny, beautiful, amazing new thing called the Internet.

PRIMITIVE Irresponsible behavior regarding finances and resources is happening everywhere. Making a fast buck is preferable to hard work. Falsely inflating numbers and reputations is the norm, and ripping off the ordinary worker is acceptable.

ADAPTIVE On deck: the reform of corrupt systems. The importance of learning how to come back from failed policies is increasingly recognized. New possibilities emerge as leaders become increasingly willing to admit their errant ways. People want to eradicate blocks of elitist decision-making and reinvigorate democracy.

EVOLVING Disciplined change can happen here. Thoughtful and deliberate reevaluation of hierarchies can be achieved. Unusual, progressive leaders can take the stage and provide more inclusive and engaged methods of reaching those who are most disenfranchised.

Uranus in Aquarius

1912–1919 AND 1995–2003

Rebelliousness both at the individual level and on a world scale ruled the day in both periods. Mother Nature occasionally came in to remind humanity to be humble: in early 1912, the *Titanic*, one of the most celebrated human creations of the early twentieth century, was knocked out of existence by an iceberg; and in 1918, a flu pandemic killed between fifty and a hundred million people.

In 1914, the assassination of Archduke Franz Ferdinand led to the outbreak of World War I; the Russian Revolution dissolved czarism and led to the creation of the Soviet Union—two sets of conflicts aimed at creating a new, better world order that had vastly unfortunate consequences for millions upon millions of people. On a happier note, Albert Einstein's general theory of relativity was born during this era of Uranus in Aquarius—what better illustration could there be of a world-unifying piece of abstract knowledge?

In 1995–2003 came the Oklahoma City bombing, the Ruby Ridge massacre, the Columbine shootings, the 9/11 terrorist attacks, the Los Angeles riots, and the burst of the dot-com bubble. Social media was born. The Taliban seized control of Afghanistan. The International Criminal Court was formed, and the euro became common currency for most members of the European Union. Economic globalization continued to ramp up its pace. The Human Genome Project was completed. In tragedy and in innovation, the world became joined more and more. The realm of ideas and information brought us together, even as we were rocked by attempts to change hearts and minds through violent attacks.

PRIMITIVE   Rebellious and egotistic behavior occurs here, with a sense of invincibility. Underdogs and outsiders use whatever means they can to get their agenda on board. Extreme movements take a grip as they push to upend the mainstream. Improbable and unqualified people seize the spotlight.

ADAPTIVE   Policies and ideas about equality sweep the cultural mind-set. People are seen beyond their social roles and are valued for their unique and creative contributions. New inventions speedily enter the collective—inventions that will shape the hardscape and landscape of the world for years to come.

EVOLVING   Genius comes alive. Far-seeing global initiatives are born. There is no limit to what is possible; everything can be shifted to a higher octave of manifestation. All previous limiting beliefs can be updated and improved.

Uranus in Pisces

1919–1927 AND 2003–2010

Uranus was in Pisces during most of the Roaring Twenties. This was the Jazz Age. In Europe, it was an economic golden age—even as radical fascist and communist political movements gained momentum. The motion picture industry hit its first big boom during this time. People lost themselves at the movies, attending films in newly built movie theaters. Celebrity sports stars and movie stars began to emerge, and with them came the whole modern notion of celebrity obsession. In the arts, this era saw the birth of Surrealism: artists like Salvador Dalí, Antonin Artaud, and Man Ray created strange, dreamlike artworks meant to express the unconscious. Alcohol was outlawed for this entire period, and true to Pisces's longing for ways to escape the strictures of hard reality, enormous efforts on the part of organized crime kept the liquor flowing.

Between 2003 and 2010, Facebook was born. The first iPhone was released in 2007. Broadband Internet use skyrocketed. In a terrifying illustration of the sheer power of water—Pisces is a water sign—the Indian Ocean tsunami hit much of Southeast Asia, destroying everything in its path and killing more than 200,000 people. Humanity sought escape from its problems through fantasy novels like the *Harry Potter* series, which became phenomenally successful during this time.

If ever there were an apt encapsulation of Uranus in Pisces in film form, it would be *Avatar*, the highest-grossing film of that decade and one of the most brilliantly beautiful, emotionally compelling visual fantasias ever created. It carries a profound Uranus in Pisces message: we are all connected to everything; those who refuse to acknowledge this may do a great deal of damage, but our oneness will eventually prevail.

PRIMITIVE Simpering, simplistic emotional memes take over the masses. Pharmaceutical and recreational drugs become widely embraced as a panacea. Zoning out and checking out combine with mass anxiety and disengagement as ways of coping with stress.

ADAPTIVE Radical quantum notions of connectedness become proven realities. You realize you are dreaming life into being and start to consciously use your telepathic, telegenic powers for good. Folks come together in mindful practices to link consciousness for the whole.

EVOLVING You see through the veil of matter to realize the sacred energies behind everything. Miracles become commonplace, and the transmutation of materials becomes normal. Psychic phenomena are available to each person, allowing all to have instant awareness of the indivisible nature of living beings both human and beyond human.

Practices for Uranus • • • • • • • • • •

Dive In

Make an outline of all the mind-bending, sudden changes in your life—both good and bad. Then, write down three life lessons you learned from each.

Reach Out

Go have coffee or tea with a friend. Talk about your wildest fantasies of changes you could make in your life.

Talk openly and uninhibitedly about a version of your life that would be freer.

Tell each other what you fear and desire most about change.

Promise each other to make at least one change and to support each other in making it, acting as accountability partners in each other's liberation.

Risk It

One day this week, wear something completely different from what you would normally wear; style your hair in a whole new way too. Notice how even a small change affects you and others around you.

Or:

One day this month, write a love letter to a friend. Take care to express all the weird and strange ways you love them and will always cherish them.

Reflect

Look at the most important social changes in your lifetime. Notice which causes you care about most or those that have the greatest impact on you. Decide on one cause you would most like to see improve in your lifetime; donate time or money to that cause.

Talking Circle Questions

Gather with one or more people who have read this chapter. Using a talking piece everyone has agreed on (see note to "Talking Circle Questions in chapter 2), have each person answer the following questions, one at a time. Make sure there is no cross-talk or side-talk; this is a time for completely undistracted, uninterrupted sharing. Before beginning, agree to keep what is said in the circle confidential, to listen deeply, to speak without rehearsing, and to be aware of time so that all have a chance to answer each question in the time available.

1. Name a time when your life was suddenly changed. What happened, and how did it feel?

2. Name a time when you chose to change your life. What was the difference you created? How did it feel?

3. Name the most unusual friend you have. How does that person add value to your life?

4. What cause do you care most about, and why?

5. What is best and hardest for you about change?

6. Tell each person in the circle one reason you would want them to be on your team if you were to dig into creating social progress.

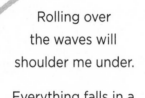

Rolling over
the waves will
shoulder me under.

Everything falls in a
tremendous shower,
dissolving me.

VIRGINIA WOOLF

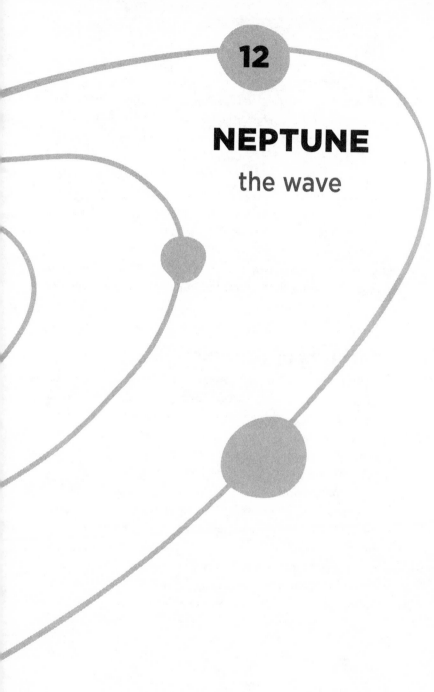

12

NEPTUNE

the wave

n psychological astrology, the archetype of the planet Neptune represents merging intuition, psychic powers, artistic creativity, and profound emotional connection. Neptune is subtle, refined, fantastical, enchanting, dreamlike; it represents transcendence, the dream world, and the impulse toward surrender—either toward the oceanic collective of which everything is a part or toward escapes into realms of illusion and delusion, fantasy, projection, or victimhood.

As it is with Uranus, the birth chart placement of Neptune gives insights at both the individual and world level. In this chapter, we focus again on the individual level of expression as we move through the signs; consider, though, how your Neptune placement is reflected in your contemporaries and the world you have created together.

THE MYTH OF NEPTUNE

Neptune, the Roman counterpart of the Greek god Poseidon, ruled both the sea and fresh water. In works of art, he is represented as a tall figure with a white beard who carries a spear called a trident; he has a bit of a temper—a destructive bent—just like the oceans he lords over. He also was the god believed to rule over horses and horse racing.

As son of Saturn and Ops (the Earth mother), Neptune is described in some versions of his story as one of the siblings swallowed by Saturn and regurgitated; other versions have Saturn tossing Neptune into the sea right after his birth. Once he and his brothers, Jupiter and Pluto, defeated Saturn, they divided the world between them: Jupiter got to rule the sky; Pluto, the underworld; and Neptune, the sea.

NEPTUNE AS THE WAVE

We all ride one unending wave of consciousness. No one survives the dying of matter and the return to the great oneness. As we mature and grow old, we dissolve, bit by bit. It is through divine grace and spiritual focus that we flow with this movement, instead of remaining encased in rigid, unyielding ego—a carapace we think will protect us when we crash against the rocks of eternity but that actually makes us more brittle and easy to break.

When we merge with radiant acceptance and dance gratefully in the unfolding of the spectacular dream of existence, we glide effortlessly within the great wave of Neptune. Knowing we are not significant within the vast ocean of time can free us to behold the mystery and surf the bliss, knowing how blessed we are simply to be here now.

NEPTUNE IN THE SIGNS

Looking at the sign placement of Neptune in our birth charts helps us understand how we and others born around our year of birth might dream, imagine, merge, and escape; how or whether our psychic powers might manifest; where and how we are likely to cast ourselves as victims; and how best we can merge with what is timeless and eternal.

Neptune in Aries

1862–1875

Through the lens of Aries, the world of imagination and dreams takes on power, directness, and vigor. In historical context, the last trip Neptune took through Aries saw the completion of the US Civil War, the eradication of slavery in the United States, and the founding of the Baha'i faith, a spiritual community that celebrates the worth and equality of all faith traditions and of all people. Victor Hugo's *Les Misérables*, Jules Verne's *Twenty Thousand Leagues Under the Sea*, and Lewis Carroll's *Alice's Adventures in Wonderland* were all published during this period.

PRIMITIVE   Lost in self-absorption, you forget that being close to others is a safe harbor. Addictions of all kinds can fester here, as the body is used as a receptacle for altered states instead of as a temple of realization.

ADAPTIVE   Martial capacities find usefulness in working selflessly on behalf of others in need. You apply energy practices to harness divine light for the community. Numerous gifts with movement and athletics can be greatly cultivated.

EVOLVING   Mastery with right action—a gift that bridges all realms of being—characterizes this evolved expression of Neptune in Aries. It brings the capacity to change matter with the mind—a divine fire of rapid illumination that transcends physical limitation.

Neptune in Taurus

1875–1888

When least skillful, Neptune in Taurus is about stubborn greed and an overconsumption that knows no bounds. For example, in 1884–1885, at the Berlin Conference, several European nations divided the continent of Africa into regions they intended to colonize. Over the next few decades, these parts of Africa were conquered, and their resources and people were used for the good of their colonizers. At its most skillful, this placement brings a sublime instinct around the creation of beauty of all kinds—both external (objects, art pieces, architecture) and internal (the soul, the heart, the expression of love in all its forms).

The sea god Neptune sent a lot of water over the earth (Taurus is an earth sign) between 1875 and 1888. In 1883, the Indonesian volcano Krakatoa erupted, and the resulting tsunami killed 36,000 people; in 1887, the Yellow River in China flooded and killed nearly a million.

PRIMITIVE Undulating with gold rush fever, you cannot escape the trance of greed. You hold on to things until your knuckles are bloody. Ultimately, you lose relationships due to your stubborn need to hoard feelings and things. Your body becomes a host for overconsumption.

ADAPTIVE You astound others with your generous giving and hospitable presence. Surrounded by sensual beauty, you are draped in a regal vibration. Your social graces are grounded in a persistent and subtle appreciation of the feng shui of environments and relationships.

EVOLVING Through the highest expression of the arts and nobility in manners, you inspire people to deeply care about the quality of their day-to-day living. Sparing nothing on making each experience beautiful, you are known for your genuinely romantic spirit. You are the magistrate of authentic beauty; you shine the light on every virtue of life's scars and its glory. Your soul is polished, smooth, wizened, elegant. You sit on a throne of philanthropic perspective, seeing that the best thing to have in life is that which you can give away.

Neptune in Gemini

1988–2002

Gemini is abstract, verbal, idea-rich, mercurial, and communicative. When its energy combines with Neptune's vast boundarylessness, it can provide for either expansive, soulful, poetic, artistic expression or a deep challenge to even organize one's self enough to speak with clarity in the maelstrom.

A few Neptunian events reflective of Gemini: in 1988, the first Internet "worm" began to wreak its havoc; the Internet went public in 1991; and e-commerce got its serious start in 1994. Google was founded in 1996.

PRIMITIVE Drowning in rhetoric and rambling half-truths, you try to convince yourself and others of ideas that hold little substance. Those who do not enter into your greater vision are expendable in your eyes. You live in a fantasy of slogans and platitudes with no mental objectivity.

ADAPTIVE Nimble and facile with new ideas, you create motivating narratives of courage and candor. Your wit and wordsmithing are widely cherished. Others are transfixed by your words and grow from their influence.

EVOLVING You can enlighten people with just the right tone and turn of phrase. Your poetic sensibilities pervade everything you do, and your learnedness is renowned. Others clamor to study with you; they recognize you as a passing flame of knowledge that is also eternal.

Neptune in Cancer

1902–1915

Neptune is at home in Cancer—both are characterized by a capacity for deep feeling, empathy, and emotional connection. However, Cancerian energy can detract here: it can be a bit childishly needy and self-serving, focused more on getting mothered exactly to one's specifications and on having all of one's mood swings and emotionally fueled opinions celebrated than on outward concerns. With the vastness of Neptune, these needs and focuses may be magnified.

Women's suffrage became active in Britain in 1906. In 1909, the Union of South Africa was established, and in 1919, Pablo Picasso and Georges Braque developed Cubism—an apt visualization of this placement. In 1914, World War I broke out, pitting Germany and Austria against Britain, France, and Russia (and later, the United States).

PRIMITIVE   Your awareness and actions are dominated by nationalistic and myopic concerns. You cannot see how anyone else has a right to the way they live if it differs from yours in the slightest. You are completely overtaken by needy, clingy feelings and the policies that spring from those feelings. No one can interfere with your moods; no one can influence the runaway storm surges of your extreme opinions.

ADAPTIVE   You are a reservoir of nurturing for those in need. You never forget people's struggles to find a home in this world. You have realized that all sickness is homesickness; we all just want a place of refuge and safety.

EVOLVING   You are a living example of kindness. Because your capacity to hold others is infinite, they can relax fully in your presence. You have transcended personal needs to create a true emotional sanctuary for others.

Neptune in Leo

1915–1928

Neptune in Leo people are naturals at creative endeavors like theater and fashion design. They have a huge potential capacity for realizing big, creative visions in a way that makes everyone around them feel loved. Skill in expression requires finding the sweet spot between cultivation of one's own generative gifts and concern for the joy and expressive power of the collective.

On May 7, 1915, the British steam ship *Lusitania* was sunk without warning by a German submarine, and over a thousand people drowned, including 114 Americans. This act led to the United States officially entering World War I in 1917.

Meanwhile, creativity flourished. In 1921, Charles Francis Jenkins incorporated Jenkins Laboratories to begin the process of developing what would become television. The first set of static photographs was sent from Jenkins Laboratories to a naval station in Washington, DC, through a telephone wire; it was then sent wirelessly back to the initial source. Soon after, moving pictures were transmitted. The modern visual art movements of Dadaism, Surrealism, and Expressionism developed during this period.

PRIMITIVE Delusions of grandeur preoccupy you; fantasies of ideal romance corrode realistic expectations. Before you make any decision, you need to know what's in it for *you*. You go to reckless extremes in the name of having fun. Your attention to self-realization dramatically overshadows your caring about the well-being of others.

ADAPTIVE Full self-expression finds a home here, and creativity and contribution make perfect complements. Others find a glee and gaiety with you that replenish and reinvigorate their vitality and sense of connection. You move through the world with an open heart.

EVOLVING You are a ray of eternal love for others to emulate. Your wildly free and affectionate nature gives others permission to be free. You are a friend to everyone you meet, and you demonstrate a palpable altruism wherever you go.

Neptune in Virgo
1928–1942

Virgo is all about service, capableness, and responsiveness. Neptune's placement here provides the potential for catalyzing mind-body-spirit well-being for all creation. During this period, science developed vaccines for some of the most feared and deadly diseases, including polio; in addition, drugs to treat infection and for anesthesia were improved. At the same time, however, the Great Depression ravaged people's health, with more deaths from cancer, heart attacks, and respiratory diseases, as well as a rise in syphilis. Individual health insurance and the March of Dimes were created during this period.

PRIMITIVE Possessed by scarcity thinking, you live a tight and inflexible life. You are overly concerned with judgments and get caught up in unrealizable notions of perfectionism. Others find you stingy and taciturn.

ADAPTIVE Propelled by the need to serve, you take great joy in releasing burdens to a higher power. You exemplify a radiant subservience to a divine nature. Around you, others are able to let go of their pettiness.

EVOLVING Like a nightingale, you sing praises to every facet of creation. Every fiber of your being hums with gratitude as you give of yourself with faith and humility. Others feel imbued with a new promise of unity in your presence.

Neptune in Libra

1942–1956

Dreaming into being the perfect partner, the potential for creating artistic works characterized by aesthetic harmony and classical beauty, and the realization of ideal relationships of all kinds that surpass any prosaic expectation: all are potentials of Neptune in Libra.

In 1945, the United States helped establish the United Nations. The UN Charter was signed in San Francisco, with the United States as a founding member alongside France, Great Britain, China, and the USSR, with veto power on the Security Council. Face-lifts, recently invented, got their own organization: the Plastic Surgery Foundation. Musical tastes turned toward big band and jazz—artists like Benny Goodman, Artie Shaw, Count Basie, Cab Calloway, and Bing Crosby were most popular.

PRIMITIVE Lost in the illusion that pretty things will bring salvation, you find yourself hijacked by the pursuit of material comforts. Advertisements seduce and hypnotize you into believing that appearances are the best indicator of value.

ADAPTIVE Seeing the beauty behind all experiences—whether ugly, painful, or ecstatic—is your superpower. You look behind the veil of surfaces to see into the heart of the matter. Your finest arts are negotiation and diplomacy.

EVOLVING   You take nothing for granted and see everything as worthy. Dark and light appear to you as a perfect whole. You lead others to embrace the totality, and you worship each moment as the ideal gift.

From an early age, Neptune in Libra Marcy read every glamour magazine she could get her hands on. Her whole life, she's dreamed of being a cosmetologist on a movie set. Marcy didn't make it to the movie sets, but she still has a thriving and rewarding practice as an aesthetician. She has beauty magazines galore in every section of her shop.

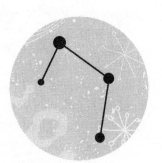

Neptune in Scorpio

1956–1970

Neptune in Scorpio people have the potential to be fearless explorers of the dark underbelly of life: sexuality, the occult, the mystical. Forays into the dream world prove more intriguing than frightening, even where dreams turn to nightmares. Explorations of loss and relationship rupture invite awakening and transformation at both the personal and transpersonal levels.

This period in history was all about sex, drugs, and rock and roll: the summer of love, Woodstock, and the sexual revolution—including sex outside of marriage and many other alternative forms of sexuality. Dark forces came to the fore with the assassinations of John F. Kennedy, Robert F. Kennedy, and Martin Luther King Jr. In this period, Alfred Hitchcock released *Vertigo*, *North by Northwest*, *Psycho*, and *The Birds*.

PRIMITIVE   Devolving into a scrum of negative feelings, you swirl like mud at the bottom of a lake. You often get lost in the pursuit of sensory pleasures. Your failure to think things through means not seeing that the known world you are clinging to is vanishing. You try to escape in all the wrong lifeboats.

ADAPTIVE   Your gift: transforming acute loss into spiritual appreciation. Aware that everything is passing, you attach gently with open arms, reserving your true embrace for total vulnerability. You teach others how to turn shame into a quest for self-love, knowing that any dark, watery cave can be lit with a bright light of compassion.

EVOLVING   You can sit with life-and-death intensity in total peace. You have realized that the temporary condition of being in a body is for the simple purpose of enlightenment. Your most developed talent is diving deep below feelings into a sea of tranquility.

Neptune in Sagittarius
1970–1984

Sagittarius represents the search for knowledge through higher education, philosophy, long-distance travel, spirituality, and exploration. Through its lens, Neptune's oceanic vastness can be directed into a refined, elegant, joyful search for truth.

The financial policies of the 1970s led to massive inflation. Richard Nixon's hubris led the world into the Watergate scandal. In 1977, Jimmy Carter created the Department of Energy with the intention of creating and enforcing a long-term energy strategy for the United States. GPS (Global Positioning System) was made available for regular civilians outside of the military. In fashion, the "dandy" looks of the nineteenth century made a comeback. Hit songs of the period included John Lennon's "Instant Karma! (We All Shine On)," Blondie's "One Way or Another," The Kinks' "Lola," Neil Young's "Heart of Gold," and The Who's "Who Are You." Diploma mills—fake colleges that confer meaningless degrees while charging outrageous fees—came into being during this time.

PRIMITIVE   Besotted with your own highly subjective belief system, you would rather go to war than admit shortcomings. You become possessed with seeking the purest and most absolute truth, and your righteousness stamps out all dissent.

ADAPTIVE   Open-minded and seeking to understand all perspectives, you breed understanding between conflicting ideologies. Your grasp of higher wisdom allows you to bring out the best messages from every viewpoint. You know how to amplify the joyous parts of any body of knowledge.

EVOLVING   You are a conduit for spiritual rapture. You connect people to the deepest meaning in every moment and offer them a way of seeing that emanates encompassing love. To others, your laughter is a song of contagious pleasure that calls them to wildly dance the dance of life right along with you.

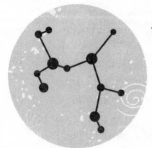

Jeannine, whose Neptune is in Sagittarius, grew up in a religious cult. She was completely indoctrinated into believing that the path she'd been born into was the only way to salvation. When she was eighteen, she met an atheist named Noah. They began to have deep conversations about the nature of belief; through these conversations, Jeannine began to question the fundamentalism of her upbringing. Eventually, she ran away to New York City and began to take religious studies classes. Now, she is finishing a graduate school program that will equip her to work as a professor of world religions.

Neptune in Capricorn

1984-1998

Capricorn's more reserved, responsible, conservative, rule-following attributes bring potential for building structures that can help make Neptune's vastness navigable. In this time in history, walls dissolved, and what was once separate was brought together: the North American Free Trade Agreement was formed, the Berlin Wall crumbled, and a new television genre—the reality show—made regular people into instant celebrities.

PRIMITIVE You are most impressed by size and numbers. You compare everyone else's statistics to your own. Crippled by your preoccupation with success, you will use any means to achieve your own ends. You do not grow from failure; instead, you pretend to be flawless.

ADAPTIVE   You are a responsible steward of resources, constantly working to improve the ecology of all kinds of systems. You are humble about your achievements and practical about reaching the dreams you and others desire.

EVOLVING   You've honed your ability to manifest other people's deepest wishes without needing personal acknowledgment. Others feel stabilized in your presence and look to you to be an ethical and wise planner.

Neptune in Aquarius
1998–2012

Visionary zeal, freedom, and independent thinking are core values of Aquarius. This placement invites humanitarian impulses and an earnest desire to bring diverse people together to actualize positive change for the benefit of all. Al Gore's presidential loss led to his winning the Nobel Prize for his documentary film on climate change. Barack Obama was elected in 2008 and brought health care for all. This placement's shadow was revealed through terrorist attacks of 9/11, the invasion of Iraq, and the collapse of the economy.

PRIMITIVE   Bohemian, decadent, and wasteful, pulled into a tide of gratuitous group revelry, you spend your days blurring boundaries in an unhealthy way. You are the last to realize that utopias are childhood fantasies, and you ask others to carry your heavy psychological shadow.

ADAPTIVE   You are a metaphysician with great insight and a diligent spiritual practice. You abide by higher-minded principles and show others how to live in diversity through a realistic celebration of differences.

EVOLVING You emit such a stellar frequency of unconditional love that others bathe in your sparkling presence. You channel fierce compassion that breaks through hard hearts and opens the community to embrace the possibility of everyone falling in love with everyone else.

Neptune in Pisces
2012–2026

Pisces is Neptune's home sign, and this is the transit in which we find ourselves at the writing of this book. This placement invites the emergence of deep spirituality as a way of life, the lifting of the veil covering our illusions, and the releasing of ego concerns in favor of a sense that we are all in this together and that we are not so different or as separate from one another as we might seem.

In this time, spirituality and astrology have exploded into the mainstream; however, the use of drugs (especially marijuana and prescription narcotics) as an escape route has become a greater and greater problem. There has been a huge uptick in unity movements, in movements focused on the rights of oppressed populations, and in other causes impacting the well-being of many (#MeToo, Black Lives Matter, Never Again). Climate change has now become an incontrovertibly serious issue, with major weather events involving inundations of water striking all over the world.

Many of us have felt weak, victimized, and dissociated as we let go of egoic beliefs about who we are and why we matter. Escapes of all kinds have enormous allure. If we can stay engaged with each other—or reengage—despite the intensity of it all, we can find far greater strength and happiness outside of our ego obsessions than we could ever achieve otherwise. We can move into a celebration of what remains—our souls and our connections to each other and to all of creation.

PRIMITIVE Life just passes you by. Numbness is the most inviting option for you on most days. Sensory overload leads to miniscule attention spans. Your norm is to be apathetic and drugged by passive playtimes. Awash in foggy confusion, you rarely find a way to marshal the energy required for follow-through.

You would rather escape into your digital device than do almost any other thing you can imagine. Indeed, that device seems to have replaced your imagination, and you just aren't sure you give a damn. You don't need your own imagination when a whole drama-soaked world is a click away—and on that small screen, you don't have to feel nearly as many feelings as you would have to feel in real life if you looked up for long enough.

ADAPTIVE As a sensational curator of mysticism and artistic expression, you amaze people with your magical shape-shifting abilities. Drawn to exquisite feeling experiences, you tap into the muses in all art forms. Empathy oozes out of you, creating a calm, peaceful pool in which others can see their own beauty reflected.

EVOLVING Transcending the time-space continuum, you are able to communicate with spirits and angels. You are a medium for others; you help deliver potent messages from other dimensions. You have come to fully understand the laws of karma, and you practice loving-kindness in every moment.

Practices for Neptune • • • • • • • • •

Dive In

Submerge yourself in water: a pool, a lake, a bath, even a shower if that's all you have available. Feel yourself as fluid and porous. What qualities of faith and selflessness would you most like to wash over you? Call them in.

Reach Out

Find someone in your locale who could use your humble help. Give to them without ever needing acknowledgment. Feel them as a part of you. Rejoice in reaching out.

Risk It

Step out of your identity comfort zone to visit a group of people you don't feel at all a part of. Notice your walls of separation; then, let them go. Pretend you are not a stranger to these people; feel how you may connect.

Reflect

What current spiritual or religious beliefs guide you the most? Make a list of the top three things you believe to be true within those belief systems.

Now, add one more belief that would let you live a life that is more relaxed and free.

Talking Circle Questions

Gather with one or more people who have read this chapter. Using a talking piece everyone has agreed on (see note to "Talking Circle Questions" in chapter 2), have each person answer the following questions, one at a time. Make sure there is no cross-talk or side-talk; this is a time for completely undistracted, uninterrupted sharing. Before beginning, agree to keep what is said in the circle confidential, to listen deeply, to speak without rehearsing, and to be aware of time so that all have a chance to answer each question in the time available.

1. Name an experience you have had that defied your former take on reality.

2. Talk about a time when you felt as though you were one with everything; describe it.

3. When have you been most deluded, and how?

4. When have you been carried away with ecstasy, and how?

5. Name someone in history you admire for bringing unity to people. How did that person achieve that end? What about their approach do you admire?

6. How do you most help others feel that they belong?

7. Tell each person in the circle what type of song they are to you: Jazz? Hip-hop? Classical? Trance? Bluegrass? Rock? Country? Choose from every genre you can imagine.

8. If people can think of particular songs in those genres, try another round in which you sing them to each other or play them on a sound system and listen all together.

Transformation isn't sweet
and bright. It's a dark and murky
painful pushing. An unraveling of
the untruths you've carried in your body.
A practice in facing your own created
demons. A complete uprooting
before becoming.

VICTORIA ERICKSON

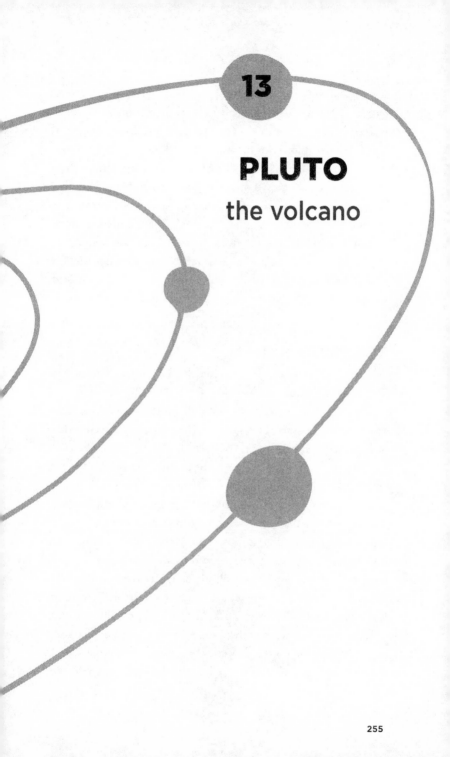

PLUTO

the volcano

Pluto was the last planet discovered in our solar system. Named for the ancient king of the underworld, it represents our deepest, darkest impulses toward sex, death, and explosive transformations. Pluto is the id—the forceful, unconscious drives and instinctive needs that often drive our behaviors without our recognizing them. Like this force within human beings, Pluto can be aggressive and dangerous—and sometimes it's exactly what is required to force a direly needed change, deconstruction, or awakening. It explodes conventions and taboos and brings both destruction and resurrection. Pluto's power is elemental, intensifying, and prodigious, and it can be channeled into good or evil.

THE PLUTO MYTH

After being eaten and regurgitated by his father, Saturn, the Roman god Pluto is said to have taken rulership of the underworld. He lived there, along with all those condemned there for eternity, behind gates guarded by a gigantic three-headed dog named Cerberus.

Pluto's abduction of the beautiful niece of Jupiter, Persephone, into the underworld is said to have given rise to the seasons: she refused to eat after being kidnapped because everyone knew that eating anything in the underworld would mean never being able to leave. She relented after several days, eating six pomegranate seeds. Jupiter sent Mercury to make a deal with Pluto to try to bring his daughter back, and it was agreed that she could spend six months a year on Earth and the other six in the underworld as the bride of Pluto. Ceres, Persephone's mother, was the goddess of crops and the harvest; when it was time for her daughter to return to the underworld, Ceres's grief caused autumn to begin, when plants would die back and the earth would go fallow; when Persephone returned, spring would come.

PLUTO AS VOLCANO

Volcanoes cool the Earth by releasing heat from its interior. Their emissions create the atmosphere and generate water for the oceans. They destroy old land masses and bring new ones into being.

The transformational powers of Pluto are profound and volcanically intense. When we access the internal inferno in a positive way, we can clear layers of emotional debris and outworn patterns. The process of metamorphosis may burn like lava; yet, the results are pure, new life, untainted by any outdated structures of personality. When we surrender to the pyre of ego death required of a spiritual seeker, we may lose identities and attachments, but the growth is rapid, undeniable, and stupendous. The sheer fire of Pluto's effect is startlingly gorgeous when viewed by the soul on a journey of rapid learning. Pluto symbolizes our capacity to die and be reborn within a lifetime.

PLUTO IN THE SIGNS

Pluto spends fifteen to twenty years in each sign. As with the other outer planets, Neptune and Uranus, all people born within a certain time frame will have the same Pluto placement, which means the sign will have a broad impact on an entire generation.

Each sign placement impacts the way in which Pluto transforms and brings destruction, renewal, and growth. No matter the sign, this planetary archetype can be called in to force veils to be dropped and false, ego-driven, or shallow concerns to fall away—to get to the real heart of what matters and what is needed individually and collectively.

Pluto in Aries

1822–1853

With the courageous energy of Aries, Pluto can bring boldness and a spirit of entrepreneurship. It can also bring a bent for tyranny and exploitation. This era in history saw the genocide of Native Americans right alongside the epic clash that was the US Civil War.

PRIMITIVE Explosive, impulsive anger, spewing without care: this is the worst of egomaniacal and unchecked power. Absolutism and aggression supersede reason. Leadership gives rise to monstrous and reckless acts.

ADAPTIVE You urge independence for those shackled previously. You take a stand to protect the rights of those who have been excluded. You stand up to bullying of all kinds with a firm and resolute stance on fairness.

EVOLVING You provide dynamic, life-changing advocacy for those who have been treated as "less than," transforming egotism into altruism. Your passionate leadership and courage on all fronts leads to highly competent inclusionary strategies and emphasis.

Pluto in Taurus

1853-1884

Taurus brings to Pluto a preoccupation with material concerns and creature comforts. On the broad historical scale, the Industrial Revolution, the end of slavery in the United States, and the growth of homesteading and sharecropping reflect Pluto in Taurus on the North American continent.

PRIMITIVE Greed and theft are the worst-case scenarios here. This placement wants to have total control of resources, no matter what the cost to others. A ruthless domination of currency and keeping most people at a disadvantage is standard policy. A belief that God favors the select few is normalized.

ADAPTIVE You understand the power of giving, and you sacrifice some so that others can have their needs met. Priority is given to redistributing resources so that most people have a decent quality of life. Feeding the hungry and the poor is a must.

EVOLVING You see the glory of beauty in all of nature and all of every species. Your acts toward protecting and conserving life on Earth are held as sacred. Your spirituality involves bringing the body to its highest, purest functioning, transcending the limits of physical laws. Others are safe in your vast presence, which goes beyond the fear of death.

Pluto in Gemini

1882-1914

Pluto in Gemini brings explosive transformation in all kinds of communication, abstract thought, and scientific advancement. This period in history brought incredible growth in these areas of human endeavor, including the invention of the telephone, the upsurge of new literary forms, and the development of quantum physics and the theory of relativity.

PRIMITIVE Obsessive, destructive thoughts with sociopathic tendencies grow here, twisting words and ideas to serve the darkest sides of the psyche. Poisonous plans and underhanded methods prevail.

ADAPTIVE Your immense ability to persuade is put to good use. Your words are infused with spirit, beckoning the mind into a space of highest good. Others are lifted from the abyss through the power of now. Great masterpieces of writing and speaking are crafted here.

EVOLVING You take your mind to new levels of consciousness and transcend the stories in favor of pure presence. You can see into the reality of effervescence and light particles and of living free from mental preferences. Others receive instantaneous transmissions of *samadhi*.

Pluto in Cancer

1914-1939

This placement brings transformations around parenthood, domestic life, the need for a protective and supportive tribe, food resources, and the overall tribe or community. The Great Depression occurred during this time in history, as did the ramp up to World War II—when nationalism, a warped and dangerous version of tribalism, went to extreme lengths that rocked the entire world.

PRIMITIVE Phobic about other identities, you hold fast to an infantile notion of tribalism, clinging to customs and traditions that emphasize magical parental figures who will solve everything. A pathological dependency removes responsibility for yourself and your actions.

ADAPTIVE Extreme tenderness and protectiveness guide your mature actions. Your own needs are secondary to the hosting of those in greater distress. Policies are developed to honor the most vulnerable and to dignify those who have had to survive much adversity.

EVOLVING Beyond nurturing and protectiveness, a divine energy emanates completeness on all levels. People soak in this awareness around you and become more able to live from abundance and capacity than ever before. A sense of interconnectedness pervades everything, and a radiance encircles all of creation.

Pluto in Leo
1937–1958

In Leo, Pluto's transformative energy impacts the worlds of entertainment (the rise of movie star celebrity), children (the post–World War II baby boom), and highly charismatic and powerful people coming into their greatest visibility (Franklin Roosevelt, Adolf Hitler, Joseph McCarthy, Martin Luther King Jr.).

PRIMITIVE Fascinated with self-promotion and self-aggrandizement, you are the "selfie" poster child. Deeply wedded to your own reflection in the mirror, you find it hard to imagine that anyone else has great value except to prop you up. Themes that direct your gaze directly back at yourself have all your attention and ambition.

ADAPTIVE   Coming from the bravery of openheartedness, all is expressed with candor and earnestness. Creative and free to explore all dimensions of play and joy, you bring people into the wonder of being alive. True love is another way of saying, "I see you and accept you as you are."

EVOLVING   A floodlight of unconditional love flows with you wherever you go. Like a child, you cherish life in every rapturous moment. Each new experience is permeated with a sacred curiosity, and others are spellbound by your affection for life itself.

Steven, born while Pluto was in Leo, grew up poor in Philadelphia. He dreamed, from an early age, of being a famous jazz musician. At age fourteen, he started working after school full-time to buy his first saxophone. By sixteen, he was sitting in at jazz clubs whenever he could. At twenty years old, he became involved with a shady group of musicians who were deep into drugs and crime. He spent some years getting lost in the underworld, only to realize that music was his true love and that there was another road for him to follow. Steven makes his living now as a guest musician for soundtracks, and he has remained sober for the past fifteen years.

Pluto in Virgo

1956–1972

When Pluto last passed through this sign placement, it gave rise to important movements toward environmental preservation; the patient, humble, grounded energy of Virgo gave those movements a powerful beginning. Pluto in Virgo also heralded a rise in the popularity of alternative medicine. In 1962–1969, Uranus and Pluto were moving through this sign together; in combination, they set the stage for the social revolutions of the 1960s.

PRIMITIVE You concentrate on every molecule of analysis until paralysis sets in. Fault finding becomes your profession, and your probing inquiries into everything border on paranoia. Neurosis becomes a virtue as every biographical detail gains significance.

ADAPTIVE Incisive clarity breeds clear directions and precise action. Whole body-mind health is cultivated, and self-help rises in popularity. You recognize that every detail is a piece of the whole, which is valuable to remember to embrace the totality.

EVOLVING You have elevated assiduous service to a graceful art form. You perform deeds of heroic proportion in humble ways and inspire others to let go of their need for acknowledgment in favor of lasting impact. Extraordinary focus accompanies long-term solutions that solve historically entrenched inequities.

Stephanie, with her Pluto in Virgo, was raised by two doctors in Chicago. From an early age, she was frustrated and disgusted by the medical system, which would steal her parents from her on a daily basis. At age fifteen, she developed a mysterious illness that medicine was not immediately able to solve. Stephanie found a holistic healing center and started to investigate alternative medicine. This led her to become a highly respected naturopathic physician; she eventually moved to Hawaii to open her own holistic health center.

Pluto in Libra

1971–1984

In Libra, Pluto's transformative mojo most strongly impacts relationships—in particular, one-on-one relationships and the communities and societies that are built around them. The time frame when Pluto last passed through the sign of Libra marked dramatic changes in the institution of marriage and in the way human beings conduct partner relationships. It saw the beginnings of the gay rights movement, a much greater openness and freedom around sexuality, a changing of sexual mores, and an upsurge in divorce.

PRIMITIVE Compelled by surface interests, *branding* and *image* become gods. You give all your weight to what others think of you, even if it is false promotion. Outside veneer and plastic surgery are more important than any inner character. You sell yourself to the latest fad.

ADAPTIVE   Propelled by concerns around fairness and social harmony, you work toward a union of ideas and interests. A born mediator, you adeptly bring out core values on every side. Your beauty is drawn from a deep well of healthy, soulful living.

EVOLVING   A master painter of gorgeous realities, you empower others to revel in their ability to visualize their greatest good. Your capacity to see into people's true motivations allows them to transform lower vibrations into more cultivated concerns for others. Radical authenticity is your teaching.

Pluto in Scorpio
1983-1995

Deep dives into secret depths and forbidden realms, a focus on life-and-death concerns, and a favoring of intense experiences—these are the stuff from which the Pluto in Scorpio transit is made. During the recent passage of Pluto through Scorpio, the AIDS epidemic hit its peak. And during a time of seeming relative peace at the end of the Cold War, foreign policies in the United States brought American military power secretively into conflicts across Latin America. There was also an explosion in conversations and revelations around childhood abuse, including sexual abuse.

PRIMITIVE   Scarification fascinates you, as do self-mutilation and addiction. The underworld of sex, drugs, and rock and roll is your jam—until it kills you. Devil worship and evildoers consume your attention. You feel like annihilation may be a blessing.

ADAPTIVE Investigating and revealing the underworld for healing is your purview. You recognize that all darkness comes from unmet primal needs for love and attention, and you seek to give victims of abuse the assistance they need. Fearlessly, you confront the overlords of malice.

EVOLVING Death does not frighten you because you have experienced your immortality in a felt sense of mind and body. Your knowing of your divine nature allows you to facilitate the rapid awakening of others through direct transmission. Your actions come from an unwavering belief in karma and the rippling force of loving-kindness.

Pluto in Sagittarius

1995-2008

Through the Sagittarian elements of wisdom, knowledge, and expansiveness, Pluto gives rise to prophets and pioneers capable of doing immense good or terrifying harm. Google was born during a Pluto in Sagittarius period; so was the dramatic uptick in religious extremism that led to the terrorist attacks of 9/11.

PRIMITIVE In realms of wildly dangerous zealotry and extremism, belief systems are used to justify cruelty and even death. Exaggerated claims and braggadocio are norms, and excessive behavior on all fronts is lionized.

ADAPTIVE Freedom for the underdogs and the uprising of indigenous peoples are heralded here. It is time to face into the wrongdoings of religious intolerance and demagoguery. Fierce compassion leads the charge, and incisive, transformational speech is used to lift the veil of partisanship. Grace is renewed.

EVOLVING   Truth and authenticity are on the main stage. There is a bell of stunning clarity for the wisdom of ancestors to be reclaimed and honored. Here, you feel that the dark clouds have lifted, and there is a future of true humanity ahead.

Pluto in Capricorn

2008-2024

As of this writing, Pluto finds itself within Capricorn's systematic, disciplined, law-abiding purview. The status quo is being disrupted, and the powers that have been in control are being called into question regarding their relevance and trustworthiness. Edward Snowden, the Occupy Wall Street movement, #MeToo, the election of Donald Trump to the presidency, patriarchy, the US educational and health-care systems, Brexit: as systems reach a point at which their artifice and hypocrisy are impossible to ignore, newer and better systems can be built to take their place. Capricorn does this responsibly and with patience and foresight. Patriarchy unquestioned has come to an end.

PRIMITIVE   The race for control of wealth is on—and it doesn't matter who is sidelined or hurt. Superiority and master race rhetoric dominate, and the rationalizations of prejudice soar. Leaders emerge who will stop at nothing to gain autocratic authority.

ADAPTIVE   Reconciliation and restorative practices are gaining momentum as people realize the cost of abject materialism and the criminality behind it. Integrity springs into unexpected places. Resistance to systems that produce economic disparity grows.

EVOLVING Spiritual leaders become more respected than politicians as they point to the emergency task of advancing human consciousness. People become desperate for real connection instead of the illusion of material happiness. Systems are designed to accommodate the needs of all members of community, beyond those of the elite such systems once served.

Pluto in Aquarius

1778–1798

Aquarius can bring a stoic detachment and abstract thinking that allow for unthinkable acts—because the emotional side of things is out of reach—or an intensified attention on building strategies for the well-being of the collective. In 1776, the Declaration of Independence was signed, and soon after came the Revolutionary War. The Federalist Papers, the Bill of Rights, and the Alien and Sedition Acts were penned.

Pluto in Aquarius is the antihero—the big-thinking reformer who is unafraid to use unique or shocking tactics to enact social change for the good of all.

PRIMITIVE Cold austerity replaces empathy. Towers of indifference are built from the rubble of broken families and dreams. The heart has been replaced with a machinelike calculator, and the icy policies of the powerful are impenetrable. Living from the steely mind allows detachment from human connection—and this detachment is what allows atrocities like slavery, prejudice, and abuse to take place.

ADAPTIVE Visions manifest to bring the globe together in a reformation of collective well-being. Leaders shift their focus toward promoting everyone's interests instead of fomenting nationalism. A deep-hearted reflection on the next seven generations takes place; people plan for escalation in human-centered values.

EVOLVING Beings from other dimensions and planets arrive and demonstrate the presence of the divine in all things. Humanity takes its place in an intergalactic sensibility. Mysteries of creation are revealed, and the human blueprint takes a leap in consciousness and conscience. A vast correction takes place for all of planet Earth.

Pluto in Pisces

1797–1823

Victimization; surrender; being in touch with visions, the spiritual, dreams—all of these color the lens through which Pluto shines through Pisces. The Romantic era, which emerged in Europe on the tail end of the strictly rational Enlightenment period, took place the last time Pluto moved through Pisces; so did the Lewis and Clark expedition, the Battle of Waterloo, Joseph Smith's visioning of the Mormon Church, and the Monroe Doctrine.

PRIMITIVE People and animals are corralled into camps for the purpose of serving masters. Those who believe they have more worth can justify turning others into victims. There is sorrow everywhere because people have lost their connection to one another and instead are subjugated by a few with a messiah complex.

ADAPTIVE An enormous swell of love takes place, which leads to people leaving their fixed ideas to help those in need.

Sacrifices are made willingly to reach people who have been cast out. Movements begin to gather all the outcasts and bring in powerful allies to create conditions of peace on Earth and elsewhere. A higher power is felt by the masses.

EVOLVING The body is finally understood as simply a skin sack around a tremendous pulsing and eternal source. Breakthroughs are made in telepathy and telekinesis, and people have immediate access to the collective unconscious. Heightened loving-kindness leads the world, and all thoughts of separation are disproven by science and felt in a resounding way throughout the galaxy.

Practices for Pluto • • • • • • • • • •

Dive In

Read the myths of Inanna, Orpheus, and Osiris. See what resonates for you about these stories. Recognize times in your life when you have visited the underworld.

Reach Out

Visit someone who is ill or who is in a hospital, elder facility, or hospice care. Bring them some of your vitality and gratitude for life. Recognize how little it takes to bring warmth to those who have lost health or mobility.

Risk It

Visit a cemetery and really read the tombstones. Write out what you would most like yours to say.

Reflect

Think about how you learned about the right use and misuse of power and how that has influenced your own sense of power. Pick out a symbol of your positive power and put it in a visible place, where you can see it every day. Imagine that this symbol increases both your influence and your integrity.

Talking Circle Questions

Gather with one or more people who have read this chapter. Using a talking piece everyone has agreed on (see note to "Talking Circle Questions" in chapter 1), have each person answer the following questions, one at a time. Make sure there is no cross-talk or side-talk; this is a time for completely undistracted, uninterrupted sharing. Before beginning, agree to keep what is said in the circle confidential, to listen deeply, to speak without rehearsing, and to be aware of time so that all have a chance to answer each question in the time available.

1. Describe a period of descent in your life and what you learned from it.

2. Talk about a time when you felt like someone had you under their thumb and what that was like.

3. Share about how issues of control show up in your life.

4. If you could transform something in your life, what would it be and why?

5. Who or what would you need to forgive to have closure before you die?

6. If you knew you could never die, what would you do differently?

7. Tell each person one quality of theirs that will live on in your heart forever.

EPILOGUE

Where Do We Go From Here?

The contents of this book can be perused for a lifetime and never exhausted. There is infinite potential here for learning and growth. But if you are anything like me, you can't wait to go on to the next learning adventure, and you should never be deterred from following your curiosity and passion for knowledge.

From here, you can go in one of a few important directions to bolster your spiritual, psychological, and emotional education. You can explore the vast wisdom contained in psychological astrology literature to enhance and deepen your understanding of this particular knowledge base. You can dive more deeply into the field of social and emotional education and read voraciously from the canon of authors now exploring the importance of relationship skills. Or you can turn to a discovery of depth psychological traditions and read such masters as Carl Jung, Sigmund Freud, Robert Sardello, Karin Carrington, Aldo Carotenuto, Christine Downing, William James, Marion Woodman, Clarissa Pinkola Estes, and James Hillman. My own path has led me to seek tranquility and centeredness from great modern spiritual authors like Eckhart Tolle, Thich Nhat Hanh, Anne Lamott, Brené Brown, Peter Levine, Jack Kornfield, Marianne Williamson, Pema Chödrön, Tosha Silver, and Jill Willard.

Finally, we are each given this moment, like a match lit all too briefly, to bring our own unique composition into its glory. We can't do it alone. We can't do it without support. And we can't do it without utter devotion and the humility required to rise from our inevitable falls and failures.

Hopefully, in this book, you have seen yourself and others with more loving and accepting eyes—eyes that have received a glimpse of who we can be when we are living in our most evolving states of being. My fervent desire is that every person who reads this book feels a little closer to the luminosity inside themselves and brings their divine spark to the rapid acceleration of a healthy, fruitful, equitable, humane life for all peoples and for the Earth itself.

Blessed be, from Sun in Aquarius!
Jennifer

P.S. Go to jenniferfreedastrology.com to get updates and treats.

ACKNOWLEDGMENTS

I would like to thank Melissa Lowenstein, who inspired me to write this book and helped me create it. She is my dear friend, my student, my colleague, and a kick-ass Capricorn with a noble and beautiful soul.

My agent, Coleen O'Shea, is a remarkable fountain of competency and caring. She showed me how a woman of true knowledge and focus can get things done with aplomb and grace.

Over the years, I have had the honor to work with thousands of clients and hundreds of students. They have been my most impactful teachers. Their lives have illuminated the way.

I have also been privileged and honored to study with the greatest astrologers of our time: Rick Tarnas, Caroline Casey, Lynn Bell, Darby Costello, Lynne Stark, and Yvonne Klitsner. I have been deeply influenced by Carl Jung, Liz Greene, Robert Hand, Stephen Arroyo, Greg Bogart, Karen Hamaker-Zondag, and Barbara Hand Clow.

My partner in work and in life, Rendy Freedman, has been an indispensable support and guide in developing and applying the social-emotional tools described in these chapters.

The gals at Goop have been my cheerleading squad, and I love them dearly. Elise Loehnen is a meteoric shower of divine light.

Finally, I want to thank my editor, Diana Ventimiglia, for resonating so deeply with this work and making it the best it could be.

NOTES

1. Richard Tarnas is the founding director of the graduate program in philosophy, cosmology, and consciousness at the California Institute of Integral Studies in San Francisco. After receiving a classical Jesuit education in his home state of Michigan, he graduated summa cum laude from Harvard; he then spent ten years living and working at Esalen Institute in Big Sur, California. He studied there with such luminaries as Stanislav Grof, Joseph Campbell, Gregory Bateson, Huston Smith, and James Hillman. Eventually he became Esalen's director of programs and education. He holds a doctorate in psychology from the Saybrook Institute. He wrote *The Passion of the Western Mind*, a narrative history of Western thought that is often used as a university textbook, and *Cosmos and Psyche: Intimations of a New World View*, a book on his discovery of and deep dive into astrology. He sits on the board of governors of the C.G. Jung Institute of San Francisco and continues to teach and lecture at the California Institute of Integral Studies and elsewhere in the United States and overseas.

2. See "An Introduction to Archetypal Astrological Analysis" by Dr. Richard Tarnas at gaiamind.org/AstroIntro.html.

3. In Western astrology, signs do not represent constellations—unlike in Vedic or Indian astrology, which is built around the movement of constellations through the sky over time (a phenomenon called the precession of the equinoxes).

4. The chapter addressing the ascendant (rising sign) does not include an ancient myth; instead, it introduces an image of the "window" to replace an older metaphor/image of the "mask."

ABOUT THE AUTHOR

Dr. Jennifer Freed is a psychotherapist, mediator, and author with over thirty years' experience in the fields of psychological astrology and social-emotional learning. Her work has been featured in *USA Today*, the *New York Times*, the *Huffington Post*, and *Forbes*, as well as on *Good Morning America* and Fox News. She is a frequent contributor to Gwyneth Paltrow's *Goop*, writing about astrology, relationships, and personal growth. Dr. Freed serves as primary consultant for the online app Co-Star: Hyper-Personalized Real Time Horoscopes.

ABOUT SOUNDS TRUE

Sounds True is a multimedia publisher whose mission is to inspire and support personal transformation and spiritual awakening. Founded in 1985 and located in Boulder, Colorado, we work with many of the leading spiritual teachers, thinkers, healers, and visionary artists of our time. We strive with every title to preserve the essential "living wisdom" of the author or artist. It is our goal to create products that not only provide information to a reader or listener, but that also embody the quality of a wisdom transmission.

For those seeking genuine transformation, Sounds True is your trusted partner. At SoundsTrue.com you will find a wealth of free resources to support your journey, including exclusive weekly audio interviews, free downloads, interactive learning tools, and other special savings on all our titles.

To learn more, please visit SoundsTrue.com/freegifts or call us toll-free at 800.333.9185.

In loving memory of Beth Skelley, book designer extraordinaire.
Her spirit lives on in our books and in our hearts.